The Philosophy of

DUMBNESS

Joseph Choma

ORO
EDITIONS
Novato, CA

"Technology is the answer, but what was the question?"

— Cedric Price, 1979

Techne Is a Possible Answer

If "technology" is the answer,[1] then what exactly is technology? Is it artificial intelligence, robotic fabrication, additive manufacturing, machine learning, quantum computing…? Words like "optimization" and "automation" are common clouds floating in this particular sky of "a" future. One can only wait patiently for version 2.0 or 2.1 to be released. So, what really is this technology that we speak of?

For starters, the word technology stems from the Greek word "techne"—which is more associated with technique, craft, or calibration than simply focusing on "high-tech" as the singular future or answer to all questions.

In 1964, a conference at the Boston Architectural Center (BAC) debated and projected how the "computer" might transform how architects practice.[2] Some of the specific tools and technologies presented showed different approaches to defining how the computer as a "tool" could be used. For instance, some tools tried to replace hand drafting (Steven Coons's Sketchpad developed in the Lincoln Lab at MIT), while other tools suggested a more bottom-up approach, such as a mathematically defined wave

motion surface by Wilfred Hoar, John Freyman, James Fergeson, and Mario Rowin of the Aerospace Division of the Boeing Company. A tool could simply be a device to augment an individual's ability to perform a particular task[3] or a tool could be more than just a tool, but an instrument-to-think-with (tool-driven approach).[4]

Drawing by hand on paper or drawing by hand on a computer screen is relatively similar. In both instances, the individual is thinking-through-drawing. It is not a completely "new" framework for how we think-with-a-tool. However, when someone writes an algorithm to define an entire geometry—that's drastically different from drawing by hand or making a physical model. It's a different way of thinking about form through rule-based procedures. That difference in how we think with the tool is important.

High-tech tools could transform how we practice, but they may or may not transform how we think through design iterations. This doesn't mean we should reject high-tech tools. However, it is not enough to just add technology and stir in order to transform how we design, build, and project new opportunities.

Just a "dumb" sketch with mathematics used as an "inspirational image" by Joseph Choma.

"There are two kinds of scientific revolutions, those driven by new concepts and those driven by new tools ... In the last five hundred years we have had five major concept-driven revolutions ... During the same period there have been about twenty tool-driven revolutions."[5]

— Freeman J. Dyson, 1996

When Freeman J. Dyson writes about tool-driven revolutions in science, the astronomer James Bradley is one of the individuals he specifically focuses on. Bradley collaborated with instrument-maker George Graham to develop a system to monitor a telescope's accuracy over time. This was the first time an extensive use of cross-checks was used to calibrate the precision of an instrument to six-figures of accuracy in the 1700s. Something as "dumb" as "calibrating" was a significant contribution in itself.

Bradley went on to make two significant contributions to the field of astronomy, including the discovery of the aberration of starlight and nutation. However, these discoveries were initiated through a tool-driven approach. Through his meticulous and precise data collection he recognized irregularities. For two years he continued to collect data without fully understanding why the data was the way it was. Eventually, he discovered and proved that the displacement of the image of a star is due to the motion of the earth in its orbit around the sun. This was the first discovery to prove the Copernican view of the universe—that the earth is in fact moving around the sun. Furthermore, he identified strange outliers in his data collection. In many ways these were "happy surprises" that initiated another new hypothesis. Then it took him 19 additional years of data collection to prove his hypothesis of nutation—the nodding motion of the earth's axis.

Bradley was not an Einstein or Newton (whose contributions were concept-driven). Overall, Bradley was invested in techne, or the craft and calibration of his tool (the telescope). It was his precision, persistence, and openness to accept data (that was unexpected), that lead to his two most significant contributions. Arguably, we could call this approach to rigor "smartly dumb."

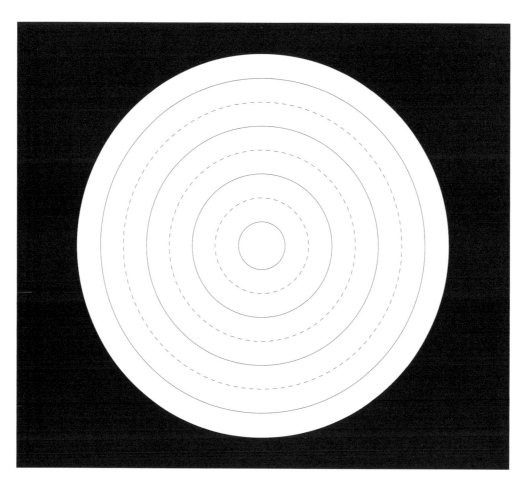

Concentric circles form the basis of a crease pattern to produce a saddle geometry.

In architecture and design, we often talk about tool-driven approaches versus the concept-driven approaches to design. Do we need a genius idea in order to start designing? I often tell my students, "If you don't know what to do, do something!" The act of sketching, making a physical model, or even writing an algorithm can help generate ideas. Similarly, if you do have an idea (or hypothesis as they'd say in science), you would then test the design through drawings, models, or simulations. The tool-based test becomes a design experiment that is evaluated and determines what happens next. Often times, the concept-driven and tool-driven are more blurred than distinct within a design process.

In many foundation studios, students are encouraged to begin a design exploration by rigorously playing. In 1927 a student within Josef Albers's studio at the Bauhaus folded a series of concentric circles on a piece of paper.[6] As the paper was folded, alternating between mountain and valley folds, a saddle-shape emerged. The saddle wasn't premeditated or calculated, it was simply the result of an exploration. Additionally, the student's initial exploration could not have been automated, optimized, or calculated with artificial intelligence, because the student didn't even know what they wanted. It was simply driven by a curiosity in dialogue with their professor. Obviously, since Albers made hundreds of paintings with nested concentric shapes (such as *Homage to the Square*), he would ask a student to try folding concentric curves.

A bullseye on a sheet of paper looks pretty dumb, but it's amazing how it results into something so geometrically complex. This reinforces Josef Albers's ideas about the "economy of design" and "minimum means, maximum effect."[7] Within this context, "dumbness" could be defined as elegance through simplicity. Maybe we need to embrace dumbness—in order to practice smarter.

It is important to mention that dumbness within this context is not referring to those unable to speak. Instead it is being used to describe something that is overly simple and seemingly trivial. However, through precisely calibration, something extraordinary can happen. Within this framework, dumbness is broken down into three parts: start simple, be irrational, and don't forget to forget.

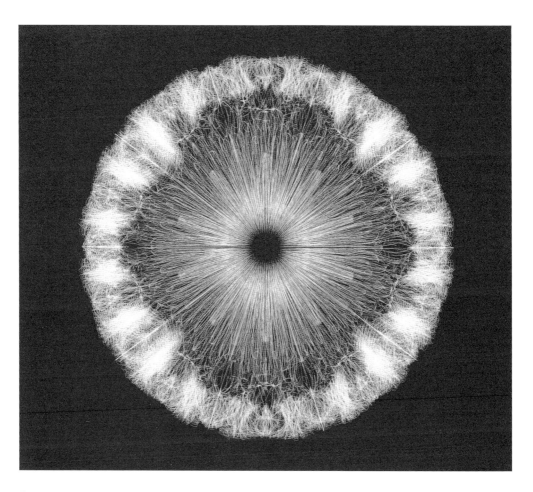

Computational drawing inspired by cymatic patterns or sound vibrations along a surface by Joseph Choma.

Start Simple

When an architect draws a perspective or rendering of a space, they tend to bias our visual perception of that atmosphere. *Dream House* (1993) by La Monte Young and Marian Zazeela is an art installation where a standing sound wave is within an otherwise generic space. If you imagine attending a concert or performance, you may be sitting in a theater, listening to the changing sounds. Similar to watching television, the stimuli are coming to you as you sit back and enjoy. However, as Ted Krueger describes *Dream House*, it is not entertainment![8] You need to be an active participant. As our body moves through the space we hear and experience complexity as our ear is the musical instrument. You would think a singular standing sound wave is just one sound, but it is the subtly of how our head tilts or how our body circulates in the space that alters what sound we hear. In some ways, the variation of sound does not exist without the person(s) perceiving it. Each individual hears and constructs their own sequence or composition. Just as the sound wave was precisely calibrated according to the room's dimensions, the experiencer's perception is also a conversation or dance between the space, sound, movement, and one's

ears. Who knew that something as seemingly trivial as a standing sound wave could be so complex!

This approach to complexity is quite similar to the way in which Sol LeWitt wrote instructions to make a drawing. A series of rules can be followed like the way a game can be played by anyone. Below is one of his drawing instructions:

"The first drafter has a black marker and makes an irregular horizontal line near the top of the wall. Then the second drafter tries to copy it (without touching it) using a red marker. The third drafter does the same, using a yellow marker. The fourth drafter does the same, using a blue marker. Then the second drafter, followed by the third and fourth, copies the last line drawn until the bottom of the wall is reached."[9]

In *Wall Drawing 797*, participants were instructed to manually record the same line over and over. Here, human error leads to a visual illusion of three-dimensional depth, all through following a minimal set of rules. This approach to rule-based procedures can also be used to inform three-dimensional geometries.

A shape inspired by Frei Otto's soap bubbles but made with "simple" mathematics by Joseph Choma.

A more practical example would be how Heinz Isler used the force of gravity to do the "thinking" for him in the design of thin-shell structures. Isler hung wet fabric upside-down, which then froze to create a surface-based approach to Gaudí's linear chains.[10] Gravity was used to design a structure that would later be flipped. Additionally, within Isler's *New Shapes for Shells*, he searches not for "better" shapes but for "more."[11] Although he embraced a "rational" form-finding process where structural principles were used as constraints to derive a form for a design, he was fundamentally interested in simply identifying new design opportunities.

A similar argument could be made for Frei Otto's soap bubbles, which were used to define tensile and inflatable structures.[12] In both of these two examples, a "game" defined by rules allowed individuals to design a form which was derived from a structural logic, such as a compression-only or tension-only system. The form was not predetermined, but was created based on "playing" the structural game the individual defined. The physics-based game did most of the thinking for them. Anyone can make a smart design playing these games. The individual playing the game does not need to be a genius, they just have to follow the rules.

In 1964, Frei Otto established the Institut für Leichtbau, or the Institute for Lightweight Structures. Duks Koschitz believes that Otto precisely selected the institute name beyond the very literal translation of light construction. He suggests that "light" could also mean efficient or effortlessness. He supports this interpretation with an excerpt from an interview by Otto.

"The secret, I think, of the future is not doing too much. All architects have the tendency to do too much."[13]

— Frei Otto, 2005

I think Frei Otto would agree that dumbness can be a means to "smart" rigor. This also relates to an acronym my second year undergraduate professor told me: KISS—keep it simple, stupid. Starting simple is an important first step toward designing smartly dumb.

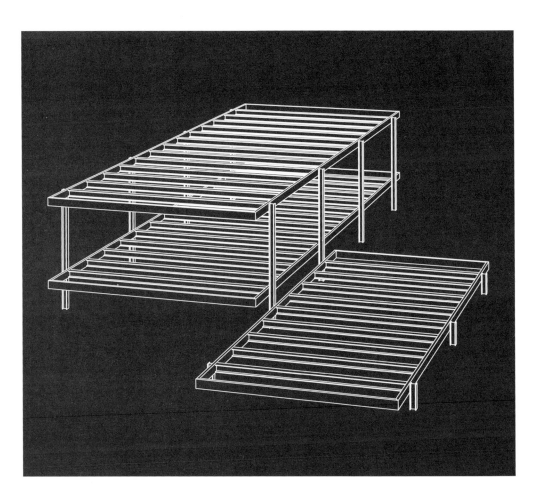

The Farnsworth House by Mies van der Rohe. Structural diagram by Joseph Choma.

Be Irrational

Stacking concrete columns and floor slabs is a rational approach to structure and construction. It just makes sense. However, sometimes architects are irrational as a means to challenge preconceived notions of what architecture is and what it could become.

In the Farnsworth House by Mies van der Rohe, a steel beam connects to a column in an unconventional and counterintuitive way. Instead of the beam resting on top of the column, it attaches to its side. This seems like a "dumb idea." However, it is precisely this detail that allows the column to be objectified and appreciated in its autonomy. This is not all that different than Marcel Duchamp placing a urinal on a pedestal. As Paul Klee would say, "Art does not reproduce what we see; rather, it makes us see."[14] Within this approach, architecture can also make us "see."

A seemingly dumb idea—which inherently might not work—forces architects to go through a rigorous process in order to make it work. Some architects call this problematizing—or to literally make a new problem for yourself—which also sounds dumb when put like that. This doggedness is what makes architecture an intellectual discourse that builds on itself. Typically, architects are not seeking an optimized solution, but the most number of possible solutions or opportunities.

Another dumb sketch with mathematics by Joseph Choma. A vortex is contained within the boundary of a cube.

Don't Forget to Forget

Often times, when we think of intelligence we relate it to memory or remembering. Commonsense reasoning[15] with artificial intelligence uses "memory" as a means to calculate. Similarly, a generative adversarial network (GAN)[16] creates new variations by morphing parts of a collection of data. For example, sampling a series of photographs of faces as a means to produce new faces. Although it may seem counterintuitive, I think it is equally important to forget as it is to remember.

"To see is to forget the
name of the thing one sees."[17]

— Paul Valéry, 1936

Typically, this quote by Paul Valéry resonates with the discourse of Fine Arts,[18] but specific mindsets or tools can also be blinding for architects and designers. Instrumentality refers to our preconceived notions of how specific tools should be used. A famous example is Abraham Maslow describing a hammer needing a nail.[19] This also pertains to design tools. For example, when given pen and paper, the assumption is that we must draw. However, if we can remember to forget how a pen is traditionally used with paper, we could use the tool in an unconventional manner. Such as a pen being used to poke holes in a sheet of paper or to roll the paper around the pen to curl the paper. Furthermore, we could choose not to use the pen at all and just fold the paper. In that instance, an additional constraint could actually open-up possibilities of seeing different design trajectories. We design and think differently when we fold paper compared to drawing by hand. Both are valuable, but they will likely yield a different set of opportunities.

The way in which children develop echoes the concept of seeing beyond that which is there. Jean Piaget and Bärbel Inhelder wrote about how children perceive the world before they understand language.[20] When a child sees a roll of tape, they may see more than the dictionary definition of the word. They may see a bracelet, a wheel, a frisbee, or something else. Initially they understand circles and squares as more the same than different. To a child, they are both closed loops (a topological relationship).

Forgetting is as important as remembering and that constructed memory (and history) can (and should) be designed. Choosing what and when to forget is an important design decision. That said, feel free to forget everything you have just read.

Building off of that which is known. Polyhedron transformation by Joseph Choma.

Notes

1   Price, Cedric. *Technology is the answer, but what was the question?* Pidgeon Audio Visual, 1979.

2   Barnett, Jonathan. "Will the Computer Change the Practice of Architecture?" *Architectural Record*, (January 1965): 143–50.

3   Choma, Joseph. *Morphing: A Guide to Mathematical Transformations for Architects and Designers.* London: Laurence King Publishing, 2015.

4   Choma, Joseph. *Études for Architects.* New York: Routledge, 2018.

5   Dyson, Freeman J. "Two Revolutions in Astronomy." *Proceedings of the American Philosophical Society* 140, no. 1 (1996): 1–9.

6   Wingler, Hans M. *The Bauhaus: Weimar, Dessau, Berlin, Chicago.* Cambridge, MA: MIT Press, 1969.

7   Albers, Josef. "Creative Education." In *The Bauhaus: Weimar, Dessau, Berlin, Chicago*, edited by Hans M. Wingler, 142–43. Cambridge, MA: MIT Press, 1969.

8   Krueger, Ted. "This is Not Entertainment: Experiencing the Dream House." *Architectural Design* 78, no. 3 (2008): 12–15.

9   LeWitt, Sol. *Wall Drawing 797*. Amherst, MA: Mead Art Museum, Amherst College, 1995.

10 Tomlow, Jos, Rainer Graefe, Frei Otto, and Harald Szeemann. *Das Modell, The Model.* Stuttgart: Institut für Leichte Flächentragwerke, 1989.

11 Isler, Heinz. "New Shapes for Shells." *Bulletin of the International Association for Shell Structures*, no. 8 (1960): 123–30.

12 Otto, Frei, and Bodo Rasch. *Finding Form: Towards an Architecture of the Minimal.* Stuttgart: Axel Menges, 1996.

13 Koschitz, Duks. "Frei Otto, 1925-2015." *The Architect's Newspaper*, (May 2015). Accessed May 10, 2018. https://archpaper.com/2015/05/frei-otto-1925-2015/

14 Klee, Paul. *The Diaries of Paul Klee, 1898-1918.* Berkeley: University of California Press, 1968.

15 Liu, Hugo, and Push Singh. "ConceptNet — a practical commonsense reasoning tool-kit." *BT technology Journal* 22, no. 4 (2004): 211–26.

16 Goodfellow, Ian, Jean Pouget-Abadie, Mehdi Mirza, Bing Xu, David Warde-Farley, Sherjil Ozair, Aaron Courville, and Yoshua Bengio. "Generative Adversarial Nets." *Advances in Neural Information Processing Systems*, (2014): 2672–80.

17 Valéry, Paul. *Degas Danse Dessin*. Paris: Ambroise Vollard, 1936.

18 Weschler, Lawrence. *Seeing Is Forgetting the Name of the Thing One Sees: Expanded Edition, Over Thirty Years of Conversations with Robert Irwin.* Berkeley: University of California Press, 2009.

19 Maslow, Abraham H. *The Psychology of Science: A Reconnaissance.* New York: Harper & Row, 1966.

20 Piaget, Jean, and Bärbel Inhelder. *The Psychology of the Child.* New York: Basic Books, 1969.

"Today's newspaper is better than yesterday's because it is today's."

— Cedric Price, 1977

An Anti-Manifesto

In the late 1940s and early 1950s, two architects designed houses with transparent exterior walls. It was during these years that an artist also painted white on white canvas, while another composed a three-movement music composition—where the performer does not play a note during the piece's four minutes and 33 seconds. Glass boxes, white canvases, and objectifying the sounds of an atmosphere are all cultural artifacts of a particular time and place.

Even though many architects have proudly stated manifestos as a singular authoritative vision, that is usually far from reality. We don't live, think, and design in a vacuum. Indirectly or directly we are influenced by others. Although "I" have titled this manifesto (or anti-manifesto), I have seen contemporary works by others that embrace this fundamental approach to rigor.

I solicited specific individuals to answer the question "What is the dumbest, but smartest thing you've done?" Each contributor was instructed to submit a text and image. No specific word count was specified, but each was asked to be precise and concise—embracing the dumbness ideology.

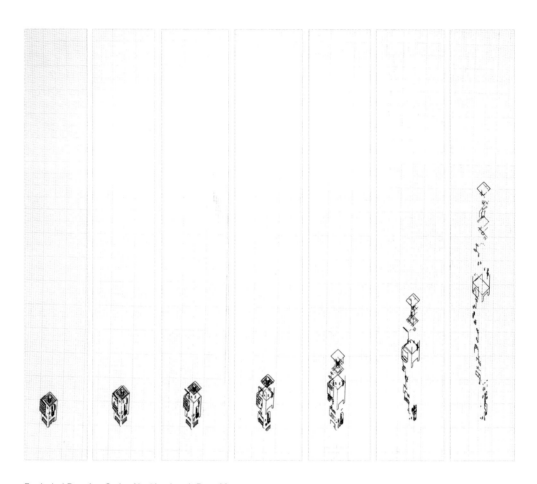

Exploded Drawing Series No.1 by Jonah Ross-Marrs.

What Is the Dumbest, but Smartest Thing You've Done?

Exploding Dumbness: Happy Mistakes Breaking a Poorly Built Drawing Machine

Frustrated with my mediocre skills at designing actual buildings at architecture school and feeling the narcissistic desire to make myself noticed by my colleagues, I hacked together a computer-controlled drawing machine from e-waste with the intention to make very narrow but infinitely long prints (without quite knowing why such a machine would be useful).

Because my machine was poorly wired, during testing it malfunctioned and produced an interrupted computer print.

After I showed this print to a colleague he immediately saw the potential to regularly interrupt a computer-controlled drawing to show the sequence in which all the lines were stored in computer memory.

The project eventually developed into a tool to represent all kinds of computer sequences to help make algorithmic processes tangible.

— Jonah Ross-Marrs

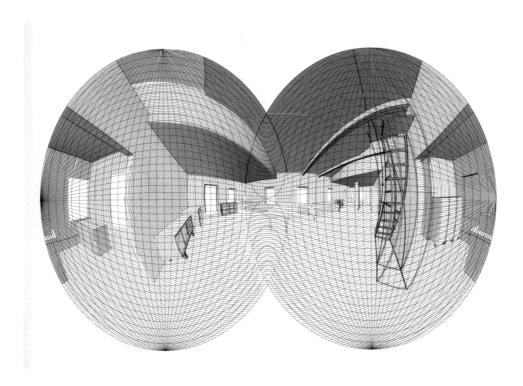

Room 27, Drawing DB-004-005 by Carl Lostritto.

What Is the Dumbest, but Smartest Thing You've Done?

Modest Computation:
Programming Drawing Assistants

Computational research often involves building systems that are "smart." We then hope to learn something about human intelligence along the way. However, in the realm of design it's hard to separate thinking from seeing. To call computer vision a "hard problem" is mammoth understatement. As a result of this reality, making a dumb algorithm can be a smart decision. When the algorithm, system, tool, or function is not meant to perform autonomously, it keeps the pressure on the human to see, reflect, judge, decide, and act. Dumb algorithms have the luxury of being project-specific, distraction-free, and easy to construct as well as tweak. They don't warrant attention, they usually aren't novel, but they can be a game changer with respect to creative agency. Take, for example, an algorithm that assists a human in hatching a drawing that is the result of a spherical projection. The computer and the human share responsibilities. The computer does little more than fill in areas with hatch lines that vary with respect to their position on the paper. All the "intelligence" rests in the task of the human, who must identify the relationship between shape, surface, depth, and space. With this kind of work, I've found that dumb algorithms can still contribute to epiphanies, but the "ah ha!" moment comes while looking at the drawing rather than while writing code.

— Carl Lostritto

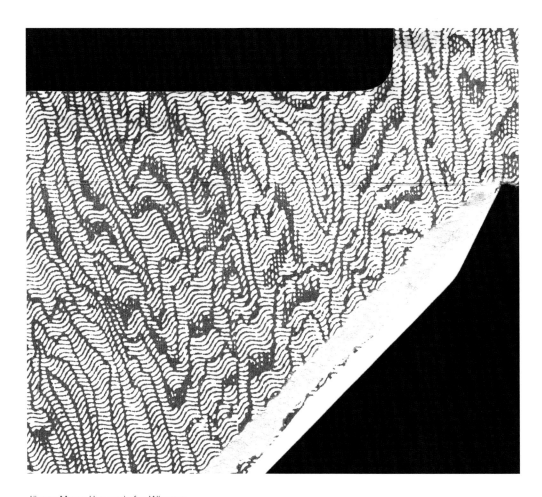

Jürgen Mayer H. sample for *Wirrwarr*.

What Is the Dumbest, but Smartest Thing You've Done?

Wirrwarr

I opened an envelope
and found a universe.

— Jürgen Mayer H.

Photographs by Robert Silance.

The Not So Obvious, Obvious

One of the dumbest and simultaneously one of the most profoundly amazing images I have ever seen is a photograph of a bare lightbulb projecting from a fire-engine red ceiling with white extension cords radiating outwards. Even this written description of the image is clearly dumb. The photograph was taken by William Eggleston, a photographer from Memphis, Tennessee. I saw it at the Museum of Modern Art in New York City. How can that be? It's simply ridiculous that a photograph as dumb as that could be displayed in such a renowned museum as MoMA. The initial impact and continued influence of that image is my "smartly dumb" answer to the original question offered in this volume.

Simply put, photography is a process of visual editing from the world at large. It's collecting images and placing them in an alternate context in order to see something different. I liken it to fishing. I have to go out into a stream of images with the proper equipment and bring back something worthwhile. In my case, dumb, or at least simply presented and clearly realized with no pretext or extraneous duties.

Within my own context the form and content or subject of the photograph should be indistinguishable. It is not just a photograph *of* something, it's a photograph. This is particularly difficult to achieve when the subject is easily recognizable. Is it a photograph of a rock, a parking lot, or a fence? Or is it something altogether different because of the way it is presented? The meaning of the image is exactly what it appears to mean. The sustaining interest and intelligence of the documentation of things lies mostly in the particular manner of their recording. The dumbness of a box of rocks is not as dumb as you might think.

— Robert Silance

Speaker mounted to a steel plate. Photograph by Ted Krueger.

What Is the Dumbest, but Smartest Thing You've Done?

The Unexpected Result

During some failed experiments to create a speaker that makes no sound (an infrasonic device), I observed some surprising behaviors in a vibrating steel plate. When activated by a constant frequency and constant amplitude signal source, the steel surface, rather than responding with monotonic sounds, emitted a variety of unexpected behaviors. Sound patterns of increasing rhythmic intensity and complexity emerged as did other effects like self-cancellation and memory. The behaviors were intimately dependent upon the spatial conditions in which the experiments were run recalling John Muir's observation that when you tug on something you discover that its tied to everything else. While for some the impulse would be to explain these anomalous results, for me the question became "Why was I surprised?" Rather than explain away or excuse the new, contemplating my reaction shed light on unarticulated residual epistemological assumptions that the signal, information, dominates the material. It does not. This is a common problem in how work is conceptualized in digital design culture. It's an assumption that is no longer tenable. It needs to go.

— Ted Krueger

Folding fiberglass along curved creases. Photograph by Joseph Choma.

What Is the Dumbest, but Smartest Thing You've Done?

Low-Tech Is "a" Future Too

"The future of building" is a common title within popular news articles. In many instances, "the" future is robotic fabrication, additive manufacturing, artificial intelligence, or some other high-tech tool. Each of these are definitely a future for architecture, but I also believe there may be other futures that are low-tech.

A few years ago, I invented a low-tech method that allows fiberglass to fold, similar to folding paper by hand. The technique is so simple that it appears almost trivial, except for the fact that no one had ever done it before. The process of folding fiberglass is straightforward:

Step 1: Start with a dry fiber reinforcement fabric (such as a cross-stitched fiberglass textile).

Step 2: Mask off the mountain and valley folds of the crease pattern.

Step 3: Apply resin on the unmasked fabric.

Step 4: Allow the resin to cure.

Step 5: Remove the masking and fold the surface.

Step 6: Flat-pack and transport the surface to the site.

Step 7: Deploy the surface and infuse the dry seams with resin.

Step 8: This results in a rigid lightweight folded fiberglass structure.

Robots are a future, but not everyone has a robot in their workshop or knows how to program one. However, anyone can learn to fold fiberglass. It is a dumb technique that is accessible to everyone. And, it is also smart! Features include the potential for numerous variations, no fasteners or molds, decrease in manufacturing costs through a reduction in production time, and zero material waste, high portability and flat-packing capabilities, and the possibility to design stronger lightweight structures.

— Joseph Choma

Thin-shell funicular concrete vault being pulled from a fabric-formed mold.
Photograph by Mark West.

What Is the Dumbest, but Smartest Thing You've Done?

Surviving Logic

Dumb.

Dumb as silent, not as "stupid," but if not stupid, then perhaps foolish, like the freedom of the Fool breaking rules. The wise old saw, "good judgement comes from experience, but experience comes from bad judgement," partly explains why the history of technology amounts to a catalog of misunderstandings and mistakes. The New is born of misreadings, errors, things dropped and broken. It is mutations that drive change—how else would the Unexpected arise?

Another important thing about a Mr. Choma's *Philosophy of Dumbness* is its love of stupefying simplicity. Insert here, image of open palm smacking forehead, accompanied by the ejaculation "why didn't I think of that!" And the answer is: because the most surprising ideas don't come from thinking. They come from finding.

My example:

Pouring concrete into a light fabric mold, and (adding dumbness upon dumbness) using only flat sheets right off the roll— no sewing, no tailoring, just flat sheets. This last constraint comes from builder culture with its allergy to procedural complications. Who knew that the flat sheet constraint would lead to an extraordinary variety of structural, architectural and sculptural forms? Who knew that asking a flat woven sheet to form compound curvatures would produce buckled surfaces with inherent structural intelligence? Who knew that the leakage of air and water through a fabric mold-wall would improve the quality and strength of the concrete? The list of findings goes on and on. Aberrant experience trumps common sense yet again.

— Mark West

Photograph by M. Wesam Al Asali.

040   What Is the Dumbest, but Smartest Thing You've Done?

Niche Problems for Transformative Solutions

We were fighting against time for a thin-tile shell installation in a ceramic exhibition when we realized that our medium-scale groin vaults require cutting each tile at the groin intersection. That was unexpectedly laborious. When thinking about developing the manufacturing of groin vaults in pieces, the available suggestions were to systemise thin-tile cutting using current technologies for precise and fast cutting. It did not sound like what a thin-tile would want. Why would one cast (or extrude) a thin-tile and then cut it to accommodate an irregular geometry while any other cast material is happy to do the job? The result is a hybrid concrete/thin-tile system of triangular pieces where concrete shapes the edges and thin-tile arches in the web. What started as a niche problem of time has ended in what will hopefully be a synergy between highly engineered concrete ribs with traditional thin-tile vaulting.

— M. Wesam Al Asali

Sofa, from "The Silhouette of Feeling" forthcoming book: Coy Howard.

What Is the Dumbest, but Smartest Thing You've Done?

Dumb

In art
Every idea is dumb
It is action that is smart

All mistakes
Made once are dumb
To do it again with intent
Is genius

Flaws,
There is no such thing
Everything is imperfect

Dumbness
Is thinking quality
Lies in only one place

Dumb
Is the desire, a step
To fluency and flexibility

— Coy Howard

Weatherizing by Catie Newell of Alibi Studio.

What Is the Dumbest, but Smartest Thing You've Done?

Weatherizing

The garage was dark; a strong and
familiar volume held away from the
light. It's normative windows were
long since gone, covered for reasons
of security. Piercing the wall was done
on instinct, a new conduit for the
exchange of light and darkness. Hole
after hole, the accumulating glow
exchanged the atmospheres across
the wall and celebrated the dark within.
It was merely a simple length of glass.

— Catie Newell

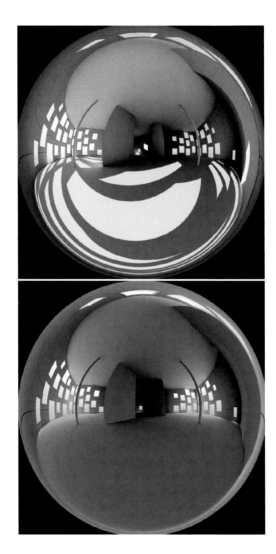

Immersive daylight renderings of the Zollverein School of Management and Design by SANAA under clear and overcast sky conditions.

Measuring the Intangible Qualities of Light

It all started as a simple question—a dumb question, really. Why do we measure lighting performance using orthographic projection (lux on a 2D surface) when we experience light and its visual effects from a perspectival vantage? After a particularly informative lecture about lighting metrics by a former professor at MIT, I walked home along Massachusetts Avenue thinking about the disconnect between building physics and architectural design. We measure units of light energy to determine whether an "appropriate" amount is present, when and where that light occurs, and whether we need more or less of it to achieve some pre-determined threshold. These units are integrated into metrics that are meant to standardize, describe, and guide principles of design. It's easy enough to understand, but the question remains: do these metrics actually help us evaluate the intangible qualities of light we see from a human perspective?

This simple question grew from a seed of doubt into a decade of experiments, proposals, and new theories. Rather than measure light as lux values across a 2D surface, my research has sought to measure compositional properties of light across the field-of-view. Using contrast and composition, I developed a new family of image-based metrics to predict pleasantness, interest, and excitement.

— Siobhan Rockcastle

Bat Tower by Ants of the Prairie.

What Is the Dumbest, but Smartest Thing You've Done?

A Siteless Start

When I received a grant to develop what would eventually become my first built installation for wildlife, *Bat Tower,* I developed the project without an actual site in mind. Keen to design the project as a deployable "prototype," I imagined that I could easily find a site in Buffalo or another urbanized setting nearby. However, despite the fact that the project had funding, organizations in the city were reluctant to host the installation. Although some organizations were interested in the notion of bats as natural pesticides and pollinators, most of the people I approached were not interested in attracting bats to their property. After a period of site-searching, I received a positive response from Griffis Sculpture Park, an amazing park full of hiking trails and sculptures, located an hour outside of Buffalo. However, as beautiful as the setting was, the location for the installation was not easily accessible by car; only a 4-wheel-drive vehicle could slowly climb the steep muddy hill that led to the site. Given this limited access, I revised the design of the project's foundation to accommodate for more easily transportable materials. Rather than pouring concrete for the foundation, I devised a shallow wooden foundation, constructed from stacking dimensional lumber in a composition that also served as planters for insect-attracting plants. In retrospect, this design constraint helped strengthen the project; the planters at the base are a characteristic part of the installation. The constraints of accessing the site also challenged me to work through a more self-reliant, nimble mode of operation. For example, rather than hire contractors (which would not have been possible due to our modest budget), I quickly learned and earned certification to operate a Class 7 Rough Terrain Forklift. While a seemingly minor detail in the construction process, this task was one of many decisions that ultimately made the project possible, and simultaneously made the installation experience an extremely memorable one.

— Joyce Hwang

Photograph by Gramazio Kohler Research, ETH Zürich.

What Is the Dumbest, but Smartest Thing You've Done?

Selbstverständlichkeit

What does dumbness mean for a robot? When asking ourselves this question the wonderful German word "Selbstverständlichkeit," for which we never found a fully satisfying English correspondent, came to our mind. While it translates to self-evident, in German it conveys more than this as it implies something that is so logical that nobody would ever question it. However, it depends on context. What is very complex and tedious for the human can be dumb for the robot, and vice versa.

The dumbness, and thus beauty and elegance of a (building) process happens when human and machine both perform something that is simple to them, meaning fully leveraging on their innate or intrinsic strengths, and perfectly complement each other. To place a brick in space, at any position and angle, is what the robot can do best, just by numerical control of its motors. Because it's just dumb.

— Fabio Gramazio

Walking Assembly by Matter Design.

What Is the Dumbest, but Smartest Thing You've Done?

Dumb Megaliths

When the Dutch explorers first encountered Easter Island, they asked the Rapanui people how their ancestors could have possibly moved those massive statues. The Rapanui told them "our ancestors did not move those stones, the stones walked themselves." For centuries, this was dismissed as stone worship, but the Rapanui were telling the truth. The statues, known as Moai, were transported standing, pivoting from side to side. The Moai were engineered to walk! For the past five years, I have been challenging myself with the ancient, but straight-forward task of moving, and standing big heavy objects. This dumb challenge is not designed to prove theories about the past. It is meant to force us to think differently about our approaches to architecture today. In an era when our default solution to handling mass is to acquire a larger crane, my work is questioning how we as architects can expand our scope—to interrogate how to better inform architecture with the challenges of transportation and assembly. While the results of this work perform tasks by rolling, rocking, and spinning with little energy, the dumb exercise encourages thinking of architecture through an alternative lens—not as an end product, but as a performance, from conception to completion.

— Brandon Clifford

Rwanda Cricket Stadium by Light Earth Designs.

Complex Simplicity

An architect is an author, a maker, a designer, someone who is supposed to have a voice. Instead of having a voice, I listen. It is smart to be dumb. I listen to the Earth, and the trees too, but mostly I listen to Gravity. Gravity has a lot to say. And although Gravity was first given voice near an apple tree, it has grown a lot since then. Of course, people were listening to Gravity before that time, often exquisitely, but without being able to precisely put a finger on what they were hearing. Gravity has always been telling us where we should put our material, based on which material we might choose.

For generations we listened. Now, with our fancy equations and computers, we ask Gravity, is this where it should go? And more often than not, Gravity says "No." But we are prone to ignore that advice and build it anyway. Out of reinforced concrete. Or steel. But with natural materials, it pays to listen, because we don't have the luxury of ignoring Gravity. And that is a comfort, because Gravity helps us design efficiently.

In Kigali, with the Rwanda Cricket Stadium, we used the trace of a ball, drawn by gravity, bouncing down a slope, to generate the initial form. We then let gravity, through the amalgamation of loads, show us where the force paths travel, and where we should put our earthen material. Because the earthen tiles are not strong, we had to aim for maximum efficiency in form, hearing the same song that Gravity has been singing for thousands of years, and letting us listen to where the loads want to go.

— Michael Ramage

A young fisherman walks under the root bridge at Mawlynnong village. In the relentless damp of Meghalaya's Jungles the Khasi people have used the trainable roots of rubber trees to grow bridges over rivers for centuries. Photograph by Amos Chapple.

The Power of Lo—TEK

If sustainability is the answer, what was the question? We commonly think of sustainability as bringing plants and trees onto buildings, but what if our most sustainable innovations were rooted in cultures who figured it out some millennia ago. Lo—TEK is how humans have been dealing with the extremes we now face, by harnessing the energy and intelligence of complex ecosystems. It is eminently possible to weave ancient knowledge on how to live symbiotically with nature into how we shape the cities of the future, before this wisdom is lost forever. We can re-wild our urban landscapes, and apply Lo—TEK ecological solutions to sanitation, storm surge, sea level rise, drought, deluge, wildfire, food supply, and fresh drinking water, that have worked for indigenous peoples for thousands of years, without the need for surveillance, computer servers, AI, or extra IT support. Will we drown in information, while starving for wisdom?

Sustainability is following the path of modernism, by manifesting high-tech, homogenous solutions with an air of superiority. As the Dutch save the sinking city of Jakarta with neo-colonial technologies, the local polder-dyke fish-ponds that are indigenous to the island and the most productive rice-fish infrastructure in Indonesia, are ignored. Specifically designed to operate at an elevation of one to two meters, the sawah tambak already embodies the intelligence of the Javanese climate, culture, and ecologies. As floating cities begin to flourish, the technologies of aquatic

civilizations who've been confronting the same crisis we now face for 6,500 years, like the Madan in Iraq, the Uros in Peru, the Kyoga, the Intha, or the Abenaki are overlooked.

The crisis of our warming world requires the entire diversity of ingenuity and innovation, borne from thousands of years of living in harmony with nature that Lo—TEK can offer. It counters the idea that indigenous innovation is "low-tech," unsophisticated, or primitive and instead aligns to today's sustainable values of low-energy, low-impact, and low-cost, producing complex nature-based innovation that is inherently sustainable. TEK, meaning Traditional Ecological Knowledge, is the cumulative body of multigenerational knowledge, practices, and beliefs handed down through generations by traditional songs, origin stories, and everyday life. In this storytelling lies an incredibly sophisticated understanding of land, technology, and practice that ultimately exhibits our potential symbiosis with nature using biodiversity as the building block for the sustainable cities of the future. Lo—TEK is calling attention to an entire body of nature-based technology that humans have evolved over millennia to confront climate change. It is a movement toward rebuilding indigenous philosophy and vernacular design to generate sustainable, climate-resilient infrastructures. The original high-tech was once Lo—TEK. Maybe it should be again.

— Julia Watson

Philippe Rahm architectes's interior design "fabrics" interact with human body heat. Image from the exhibition *The Anthropocene Style* at San Francisco Art Institute, 2018.

What Is the Dumbest, but Smartest Thing You've Done?

Climatic Architecture, Meteorological Urbanism

Architecture is the art of building climates.

The object of architecture is space, that which is subtracted from the general space of the earth's atmosphere. Space is contained between four walls, a floor, and a ceiling. Only in this way, only by confining a certain volume of air, will we be able to modify the physical characteristics of the air (temperature, hygrometry, speed, and the nature of the gases) and light (visible light, infrared, and ionising and non-ionising radiation) with the aim of making this space habitable for humans, when all around the natural space is too hot or cold, too rainy or snowy, too humid, too sunny or dark—uninhabitable.

Humans inhabit the invisibility of the air and not the visibility of the walls.

The purpose of architecture is the hollow of the space we enter and not the full extent of the walls, which remains inaccessible to us.

Through art, architecture modifies a portion of the natural climate, watering down a certain amount of the earth's atmosphere, anthropizing a natural space.

The *raison d'être* of architecture is to make a climate artificially habitable when this climate is naturally uninhabitable for humans.

The mission of architecture is to modify the physical parameters of this climate to make it habitable for humans.

The whole art of architecture is to elaborate thermal, hygrometric, chemical, and electromagnetic measurements.

The architect must draw climates rather than geometric forms.

Architecture must *be* rather than say, it must shelter rather than signify.

Architecture says nothing, means nothing, tells nothing. It is only qualified in terms of variations in intensity, physical, electromagnetic, chemical gradations.

Architecture is silent. It is a background, a landscape of varying thermal, luminous and hygrometric intensities, in front of which our freedom is exercised.

Today, architects and urban planners must reinvent the modalities of their discipline in the face of the violence of global warming and its hot and polluting auxiliaries. The structuralist / postmodern modes of design must give way to the climaticist / new realism reasons. It is then necessary to go back to the climatic, energy and health fundamentals of architecture and urban planning, the urgency of which today is mainly this: overcoming dependence on fossil fuels, reducing CO_2 emissions, and countering heat waves and air pollution.

— Philippe Rahm

As the waters of the river recede in October after the monsoon, a megacity is built in under 60 days to exist only for 55 days. After the festival is over in March, the material is recycled and the site offered back to the river to occupy, when the monsoon floods the terrain in July. Photograph by Dinesh Mehta.

What Is the Dumbest, but Smartest Thing You've Done?

Impermanence

When we spent two years photographing, drawing, analyzing, and writing about an ephemeral megacity we wondered if it was a smart idea? We were studying the biggest public gathering on the planet— the *Kumbh Mela*, which is a Hindu festival that manifests itself in the form of a megacity, at the confluence of the Ganges and Yamuna rivers in India. This gathering is held every 12 years serving approximately 7 million people who gather for 55 days and an additional flux of 10 to 20 million people who come for 24-hour cycles on the five main bathing dates. Once the festival is over the megacity is disassembled as quickly as it was deployed reversing the constructive operation, disaggregating the settlement to its basic components and recycling a majority of the material used. We wondered if this academic endeavor was a dumb idea? What is the relevance of capturing what exists for a fleeting moment and not even replicable or perhaps barely tangible. One sometimes wonders if this megacity actually existed? But everyone engaged in making this city was amazingly committed as well as completely aware that they were investing enormous energy in something that would disappear in under two months. In retrospect, we realized its lessons were profound. We understood that its makers deeply believed change is the only constant and uncertainty the only certainty. Then you realize it was the smartest thing that could be done— learning that permanence does not matter. This frees you from the weight of time, challenges you to touch the earth lightly, and introduces you to the fantastic world of reversibility—a priceless lesson for an architect today.

— Rahul Mehrotra

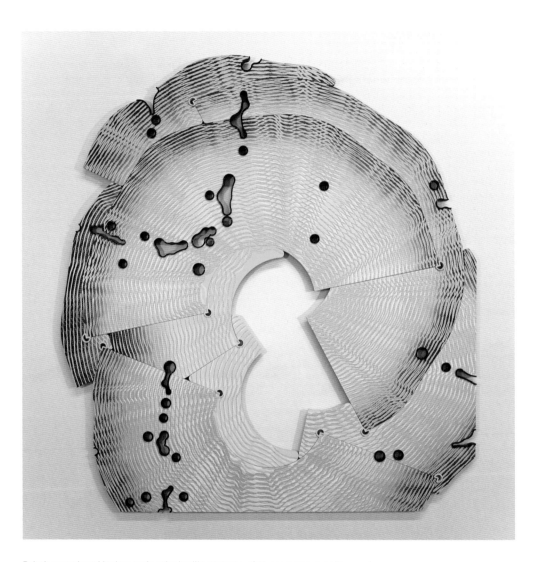

Painting produced by harvesting the bodily gestures of 21 anonymous online workers.

Architecture's Products

It's dumb to think about architectural labor; to focus less on what's being made and more on the structures and technologies through which the work of making architecture occurs. Or rather: to make the assertion that what we think of as architecture is at once the design of so many buildings, and the design of increasingly vast organizations of bodies, policies, and technologies that make any building possible in the first place. But in slightly different terms, labor itself might be understood as dumb. By this I mean that these global arrangements of workers, office protocols, and financial instruments make possible the highly visible artifacts of our discipline in relative silence. And it's precisely the invisibility of labor that allows architecture to straddle its exceptional position between an artistic discourse and a service profession.

Perhaps it's also smart to think about architectural labor; to argue that these mostly invisible sites of production might also be where architecture's disciplinary politics are actually fabricated. Where the edit permissions of popular software platforms disentangle creative authorship from the bodily labor of drawing set production. Through office protocols, software suites and drawing standards, the discipline continually manufactures a kind of politics that has less to do with the aesthetic politics of architectural objects, and instead with the material politics of life in an age of globally distributed architectural labor. In short, what if instead of organizing labor so as to realize evermore novel architectural objects we were simply to imagine architecture as the production of objects in ways that require new politics of labor, and in turn, more hopeful ways to organize ourselves and others.

— Curtis Roth

Sketch by Stefan Behnisch of Behnisch Architekten.

What Is the Dumbest, but Smartest Thing You've Done?

"Mismatch" or Process of Dumbness

Everybody knows what it is like: you are in a hurry to do your shirt up. You are still sleepy. When you look in the mirror you notice that the buttons are in the wrong holes. Unfortunately, you only realize this when you get close to your collar button. But now it's too late, and you are in a mess without warning. There is no remedy, no solution. It doesn't help to open just one button. No, you would have to unbutton the shirt over its full length and start all over again. This phenomenon occurs in all spheres of life. And that includes architecture and the process of building.

There are projects where most things go wrong, from the very outset. Everybody then tries to get things right, remedy the symptoms, or, to return to my metaphor, fiddle with one button.

When designing something, you make one step after the other. There are logical processes starting with the wish to build something through briefing, programming, selecting the design team, ideas, concepts, design, planning, details, tendering, construction, etc., to the finished building. It's like a chain, where all elements are linked with each other, building up on each other.

Often, clients or their consultants want to know and determine things long before they are on the agenda. And this is where the tragedy begins. Costs are discussed long before a concept, not to mention a design, has been adopted. These budgets are bound to be wrong. And wrong numbers are sticky.

This is the glorious moment for so-called value engineering processes. Adhering strictly to the teachings of the most up-to-date professional training course, they are "celebrated" like religious acts—but, in most cases, without a result. Ingredients such as risk assessment studies prepare the scene for risk management strategies to add salt to the soup. This, too, is an operation carried out with almost religious zeal.

After long debates and, in most cases, arguments about fundamental discrepancies, it is decided to revise former plans, just to bring the meeting to a close. At this point one realizes that the current trend toward sharing responsibilities is absolutely detrimental to architecture.

Our practice had once done a project where we knew from the very beginning that something would go wrong, or, to come back to our story, the shirt would not be buttoned properly. During the competition colloquium, it had already become obvious that it would be impossible to work with this client. We should have gotten out of this shirt at that time. But as we all know, hope dies last. Now it is buttoned wrongly and it is too late to put it right. There is no new beginning, for anybody. The building turned out fine, but the toll it took...

— Stefan Behnisch

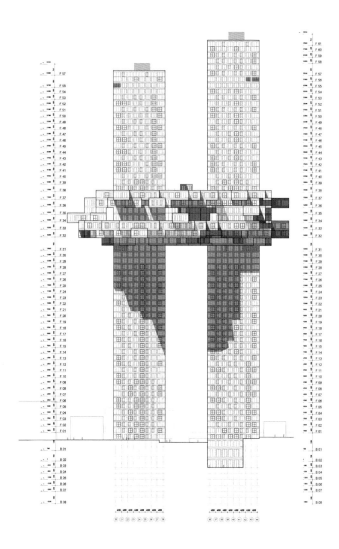

Sky Village for Yongsan Dream Hub corporation by MVRDV.

What Is the Dumbest, but Smartest Thing You've Done?

How I Sparked Outrage

At MVRDV we love working on our designs. We like to involve clients, stakeholders, and experts from a wide range of fields from early on in the creative process. We don't settle for less than exemplary, outspoken projects that enable our cities and landscapes to develop toward a better future.

Or so, this is our ambition. Sometimes, when we are designing, we can be so caught up in the creative process that we are unaware of public sentiment. Like with a work of art, architecture can be interpreted in many ways, and sometimes this is just beyond our control. In 2011, MVRDV won a skyscraper project in Korea, which consisted of twin towers connected at their center by a "cloud," an 11-story pixelated volume. The design was very well received in South Korea. "It's art," wrote Chosun Biz, and the Cosunillbo proclaimed the apartments in this high-rise for Seoul's business district the "hottest" in the area. In Europe the cloud connecting the two towers was praised as a unique architectural feature.

The press reactions in the US were a little different; New Yorkers in particular felt that the project resembled the exploding World Trade Center, and that the design mocked the victims of this terrible tragedy. Fox News—the first time MVRDV was featured here—declared us as the "worst person." "Seoul's new tower seems familiar, and not in a good way," Curbed wrote. We sparked outrage, because the high-rise was interpreted as 9/11 frozen. Dumb? Maybe, but I never intended it to be disrespectful.

The consequences were severe; Facebook closed MVRDV's account, we received threats of people who wanted to beat up the "Bin Laden lovers." Given the volatile perception by American media, we apologized for causing concern, and promised to re-evaluate the design.

This "dumb thing" was honestly one of the nightmares of my career. We feared we would never work in the United States. But the story doesn't end here, luckily; we invited the BBC and prominent Dutch media to explain our side of the story. Where others saw exploding towers, my intention was the opposite; these towers were leaning toward each other, more kissing and hugging than anything else. I connected the building to create more space for people to live in. This had many benefits; stability, an escape, the possibility of more gardens and more informal meetings. The interpretation was mostly due to a terrible coincidence and was never spotted during the design process.

Meanwhile our Korean client didn't seem to be concerned with the controversy. They didn't see the resemblance, and the client was even pleased with the publications. As things go, the controversy slowly disappeared. A few months later our media analysis showed skyrocketing numbers, we had even made it to CNN. Yes, it left us with a few scars, but only a few short months after, we began our first built project in New York.

— Winy Maas

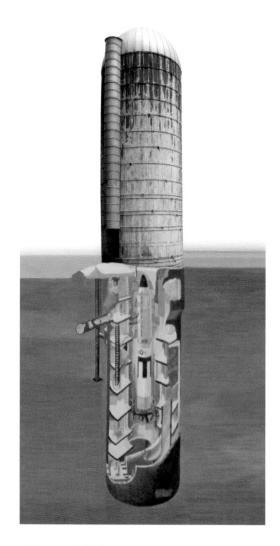

SILOs by SILO AR+D.

Get a Job

Rather than a thing, I'd offer a trajectory—
becoming professional, starting a firm,
getting a client, and signing a contract—
as the dumbest smart thing we've done.
Putting architecture's internal dialogue
at risk, in the public realm, under scrutiny,
in practice, is the most vivid way to
understand the discipline's limits and
possibilities. More than any other
medium, the contract structures
the politics of enactment, between
constituents, owners, contractors, and
architects, and has made us rethink our
practice's attitudes about authorship,
control, audience, and appearance.
Because we decided to start a firm, get
a job, and build, we no longer simply
view the product of architecture as
things, but see practice as the object—
an organization whose goal is to
produce a body of work.

— Marc Manack

The Prairie House by Herb Greene. Photographs by Julius Shulman.

What Is the Dumbest, but Smartest Thing You've Done?

The Prairie House: Disrupting Divisions within Space and Time

Our physical, mental, and temporal awareness is guided by predictable rhythms of naturally occurring phenomena that ultimately form our relationship to space and time. One of the most fundamental goals of architecture is to provide orientation between place and people. When I built the Prairie House in 1961, it was commonly assumed that repetitive design principles could be universally applied to any location and user. I was compelled, throughout my education under Bruce Goff and in my own practice, to design architecture that uniquely responds to physical, cultural, and historical contexts. Exploring relationality allows us to discover intersections between the physical and existential world. I was greatly influenced by Alfred North Whitehead's philosophy of the extensive continuum and his assertion that any event in the universe can be related to aspects of any other event. The form of the Prairie House attempts to lean into the realm of memory and experience by referencing many things, while imitating no one specific thing. The design concept integrates multiple perspectives in order to engage a sense of harmony and continuity.

The Prairie House design is an investigation of form and materiality in relation to site. The structure disrupts conventional divisions by addressing perceptual complexity within a single organic form. I chose to wrap both the interior and exterior in cedar shingles to create a feeling of warmth and to animate the entire space with suggestive movement, reflective of the natural environment. The continuous shingle placement was arranged in irregular patterns in relation to the indigenous grasses, ravines, and prairie creatures in the surrounding landscape. The cedar boards and shakes unite exterior and interior, converging with a large elliptical window that becomes the watchful eye within the "head" of the house, facing west toward the direction of prevailing winds and tornadoes. The orientation of the head is meant to express yearning and protection, as it hovers over the land, while simultaneously trying to free itself from it.

The Prairie House design creates a sense of boundless space by collapsing perceptual divisions between exterior and interior. Pavel Tchelitchew illustrated this beautifully in his painting *Hide and Seek*, by inverting figure-ground relationships to illustrate a sense of transformation in space-time. The phenomenology of disorientation may not seem controversial now, but it has been historically under-valued by more common architectural design methodologies. Regardless of era it is worth acknowledging that architecture should always respond to its place and moment. Today more than ever we need to reconcile the role of architecture within the natural environment and align our needs with those of a living planet.

— Herb Greene

The House of Three Trees by JK-AR. Photograph by Rohspace.

What Is the Dumbest, but Smartest Thing You've Done?

The Beauty of Dumbness: Wooden Bracket System in East Asian Timber Structures

The House of Three Trees is the realization of a fantasy, which began with a dumb idea. The idea is about an alternate reality in which several historical events of the past century have not occurred. What if timber resources were not depleted in the late Joseon Dynasty of Korea in 17th to 19th centuries? Despite the exhaustion of timber, what if globalization had begun earlier and had introduced the import of wooden materials from Russia, Canada, and Northern Europe as affordably as it is now? Then, the timber buildings of East Asia may have continued to evolve. These premises can give us an opportunity to retain a culture of timber architecture that we had kept for at least 1,500 years, and may further lead us to experience a new architecture.

The house is the rebirth of East Asian timber architecture that disappeared 100 years ago. More specifically, the project is the reinterpretation of the iconic wooden bracket systems ubiquitous in the East Asia timber architecture. Known as "dou-gong" in China, "to-kyou" in Japan and "gong-po" in Korea, the system was merely made of the combination of joinery between discrete wooden members. Nevertheless, the bracket system is the most iconic part of East Asian wooden buildings in both structural and aesthetic aspects. Structurally, the system works in a critical capacity by connecting the roof structure, columns, and beams into a single system able to evenly distribute vertical and lateral loads and assuring continuous load paths to the base. Aesthetically, the system gives distinct three-dimensional effects at the transition from roof to wall, through the complex assembly of wooden elements and precision joinery. One simple system becomes the most critical part of a building. This is the beauty of a wooden joinery. It is the beauty of "dumbness."

— Jae Kyung Kim

Melbourne School of Design by NADAAA and John Wardle Architects. Photograph by Peter Bennetts.

What Is the Dumbest, but Smartest Thing You've Done?

Tectonic Inversion: "Upside Down at the Bottom of the World"

Upside Down at the Bottom of the Earth, (by David Allen chronicling a brief but tumultuous sojourn of D. H. Lawrence in Australia) serves as a literary device that unleashes a tectonic inversion that is seemingly irrational, yet smart in confronting the challenges we faced in the Melbourne School of Design.

The commission promised a new programmatic element that the school had lacked over its illustrious academic history: a dedicated studio space; yet, within a month of the design launch, budget cuts eliminated this core programmatic mission.

Our proposal for the "studio hall" was a response to this very predicament. Composed of three key programmatic features, the promise of the strategy was to reconceive the studio as a flexible dynamic space, in effect not so much accepting defeat, but instead adopting the radical austerity as a means of invention. The first strategy was to draw funding from the FF&E budget to create a "hot" infrastructure of furnishing at the edge of the great hall; this infrastructure becomes a vehicle to eliminate the expected railing the edges would otherwise have necessitated. The second strategy was to create a flexible ground plane to accommodate everyday study, social life, lectures, and conferences, as well as formal critiques and reviews.

This set the stage for the third strategy. To ensure the flexibility of the ground, we conceived of an inverted tectonic system that would suspend three dedicated studio spaces from the roof structure such that they hover over the great hall. Conceived of as an LVL coffered ceiling, the wood members span over 22 meters, using the angles of the cross-bracing to protect the interiors from direct sunlight. In turn, the surface of the coffering system of the horizontal span wraps down the surface of the vertical enclosure of the totemic structure. Massive at the top, the coffering is over three meters deep; as structural logic would have it, the thickness of those members can diminish as they descend floor by floor, with massive rusticated carving at the top and thin veneers of plywood at the fringe of its bottom. Borrowing from its classical antecedents, the structure respects representational intuition of a palazzo, but here turned upside down at the bottom of the world.

— Nader Tehrani

Sketch of the Mercedes-Benz Museum by Ben van Berkel of UNStudio.

What Is the Dumbest, but Smartest Thing You've Done?

Levels of Complexity

The dumbest, but smartest thing I've done was proposing to the client of the Mercedes-Benz Museum in Stuttgart that we could design a three-story building that actually comprised nine levels. I thought it would be easy, but at first they didn't believe it could work. To convince them, we had to make multiple models that demonstrated how two spirals could be intertwined over three storeys, and repeated twisting structural elements along these spirals would enable the creation of three exhibition levels per story. The result is that from the outside, the building appears to be three floors high, however, when you go inside, you discover it is much more complex and layered. But this is not the only dumb idea we've had. While it admittedly doesn't make our lives any easier, it's actually our standard approach, because we believe that if you are not critically, or optimistically naïve, you can't innovate.

— Ben van Berkel

Vortical Filament: Spinning DC motors, fishing line, and a fishing weight—very carefully controlled.

What Is the Dumbest, but Smartest Thing You've Done?

The Immanence of Oscillatory Collapse: Reflections on Tweaking Vortical Filament

We have all lived through a moment of the imminence of a collapse. Not the predictive and studied conclusion that a technical ensemble will fail, but rather in the interstices of the very moment of an event stripped bare to an interaction of a body and a machine. I must stress here that it is an interval of collapse, rather than an assembled sequence of events. In fact, it is a moment without any apparent sequence—a moment where the senses are most heightened while logic is most dulled. Moments such as the deep and profound vibration of a spinning tire against pavement or the compounded aggression and stuttering rhythm of a blade heaving at the blurred and ghostly shape of a spinning extrusion.

The interval is a delicate marker of resonance at the moment of a phase change. It is a short interval. Even with the most complex, predictive, and contrived mechanical interventions that intercede in this moment of change, there will always be this critical moment, this extended space of enacted dexterity. If it is measureable (and neuroscience certainly is), then it is somewhere in the range of 500 milliseconds. In this moment, affect resides in an autonomous interval on its own, without context or boundary. This is just enough time for an embodied gesture absent of thinking.

Regardless of our clever interventions, it is impossible to truly know the duration since the interval is too fast for higher functions to decode. More appropriately, we should just acknowledge it as a moment when we finally cede to the domain of the senses, the electric signals of skin to habitual gesture. That interval is short, violent and demoralizing at first, and it resounds with the suddenness of a bodily ignorance. But then, to live in that moment is where we find our artistry. In fact, the ambition is to prolong this interval, resist its conclusion and embed ourselves within a sphere of material immanence where harmonics, beat, phase changes, levitation, catenary geometry, and synthesis reside. This moment strips the technical object of all its immediate, future and past concretizations and material shadows. As much as we attempt to mechanize the certainty of this chaotic interval, there will *always* be this zone of immanence to contend with. Inevitably, it will always fall to interplay between machine and body. While the interval can be contrived with the fastest and most complex of engineered controls, there will always be this potential interval where potential and chaos meet.

— Patrick Harrop

Collage of 16 images (14 photographs and two renderings) depicting spaces designed by Zaha Hadid Architects, in different cities around the world.

What Is the Dumbest, but Smartest Thing You've Done?

(A)Voiding

The idea could not be simpler: All buildings, especially towers, become, to a large extent, empty and hollow (i.e., we must substitute usable floor surface with voids for vistas). These spaces express and facilitate the complexity, dynamism, and communicative intensification of urban life in our 21st-century network society. In our designs buildings become porous and urbanized on the inside, allowing for increasing inter-visibility between the diverse social activities brought together, to facilitate browsing navigation and to maximize co-location synergies.

The motivation to move into cities, ever larger and denser, and into ever-larger buildings is clear: we come together to network, to synergize knowledge, to exchange, and to cooperate. The built environment becomes an information-rich, empowering, and exhilarating 360-degree interface of communication—a networking machine. However, it thereby also becomes an experience machine. Lose yourself and discover yourself!

— Patrik Schumacher

2014 Helsinki Guggenheim proposal by Mark Foster Gage Architects.

What Is the Dumbest, but Smartest Thing You've Done?

When Philosophy Becomes Fun

Sometimes in our office we make leaps based more on intuition rather than sound reason or some previously outlined ambition. Even wild leaps—that may be considered "dumb" in that they are uninformed by reason, but not "dumb" in the sense of not valuing or rejecting truth or information. An example of this in our office would be the language of "Kitbashing" that we developed in 2014. At the time I was reading a lot of Bruno Latour and Graham Harman's work—both of whom refer to "lists" or "listing" as intellectual devices that work differently than sentences with grammar. For instance, I can list for you "eggs, milk, fruit, bread, broccoli, paper towels, and ice cream"—and you can probably intuit that it's a shopping list. However, this isn't done with any grammar or interconnectivity of parts in the list itself, the "combining" is done in your mind. That is to say there is no "structure" for a list, or grammatical rules, but information can be conveyed. It's not about interconnectivity as much as it is about each word being independent and untethered. And yet information can be transferred.

At the time I was having an ongoing debate with Patrik Schumacher, regarding the over-reliance of Parametricism on the narrative of interconnectedness—and looking for a way for architecture to reclaim its object-status rather than merely being something composed of interconnected systems. That doesn't mean that architecture isn't composed of interconnected systems—only that conceptually I think there's value in considering architecture independent of its interconnectivity—so that it can be considered aesthetically. I have written quite a bit about this elsewhere—but the first design response I had to these ideas was to make a building with components that didn't have *any* relationship to each other whatsoever—tectonically, formally, or symbolically. So I had people in my office start downloading 3D objects from various online sources, and we composed them into a building—thus our Helsinki Guggenheim proposal—and the birth of digital kitbashing I think. This project is funny to look at—a collection of bears, toasters, rockets, mermaids, chairs, cars, and Mjölnir (Thor's hammer). I'm sure you recognize the list strategy here—and architecture of listing. It is not, nor has it ever been my intention that the world should look like this building, or that anyone copy the strategy—this was really a philosophical idea explored through architecture. It was a playful and intuitive leap from philosophy into architecture that produced something that didn't exist before—something new. This has since developed into what I would call a much more sophisticated language in some of our projects, but it had its roots in a kind of playful leap of faith from ideas into form.

— Mark Foster Gage

2017 Tallinn Biennale Installation by Gilles Retsin Architecture. Photograph by NAARO.

In Part Whole

It's probably a pretty unsophisticated idea to consider a discrete architecture— an architecture that has no whole but only consists of parts. It seems blunt, boring, stupid, and against the discipline—haven't we always been about the whole? The often-heard comparison between discrete parts with LEGO doesn't help—who would want to reduce our profession to blocks? However, it turns out that this blunt approach, this slightly stupid question, could be highly productive, both in terms of efficiencies, economies, and aesthetics. Parts are serialized, but function and scale agnostic—not unlike pixels or voxels. They have no meaning, no history, no reference. They can be automated, mass-produced, recycled, and traded without the whole. This results in a new kind of architecture, which is raw, primitive and discrete, accessible and versatile, authored and generic, unique and repeatable. Diffused by the autonomy of the parts, the whole is no longer present. Similar to the primitive hut or cave, a serial operation of the same material, assembly, process, and part defines everything, over and over. While architects interested in digital technologies relentlessly attempt to outsmart architecture with all kinds of AI's, autonomous machines, or new materials, the discrete is perhaps just the project to calibrate automation with the blunt and primitive, granular nature of architecture, before accelerating it.

— Gilles Retsin

Hedracrete by Masoud Akbarzadeh, Mehrad Mahnia, Ramtin Taherian, and Amir Hossein Tabrizi.

What Is the Dumbest, but Smartest Thing You've Done?

Smartly Dumb Geometry

Disintegrating the design from the performative qualities of an architectural geometry is dumb. Surprisingly, there exist ancient geometric techniques for the design of high-performance architectural geometries. These methods are called the geometry-based structural design methods, more concisely Graphic Statics. Graphic Statics (GS) methods originated in the pre-digital era and continue to be used and developed even today. In this method, both the geometry of the structure and its force equilibrium is represented by two geometric diagrams called the form and the force, which is dumbly smart. These diagrams are reciprocal, i.e., geometrically dependent and topologically dual. Unlike any other structural design technique, a designer can design the geometry of the force diagram instead of the form and guarantee the equilibrium of the resulting structure. The structures designed by GS-based methods are among the best examples of innovative use of material and efficiency, and many eminent engineers and designers such as Guastavino, Maillart, Eiffel, Koechlin, Nervi, and Dieste constantly used graphic statics in the design of their masterpieces. In 2016, I was among the first who developed an extension of graphic statics in three-dimensions based on a 150-year-old publication in *Philosophical Magazine*. In this method, the equilibrium of the forces in three-dimensions is represented by closed polyhedral cells with planar faces. Each face of the force polyhedron is perpendicular to an edge in the form diagram. And the magnitude of the force in the corresponding edge is equal to the area of the face in the force polyhedron.

Hedracrete is a prefabricated, concrete polyhedral structure and the first manifestation of 3DGS methods. The structure has a funicular polyhedral geometry with combined compression and tension members. The configuration of tension and compression pushes the boundaries of using concrete in the construction of spatial structures. The 2.1m³ of fiber reinforced concrete is distributed in 50m³ of space in a funicular configuration with a capacity of transferring 102 tons of external loads to the supports.

Since the magnitude of the internal forces in 3DGS is represented by the area of the polyhedral faces in the force diagram, the optimization process only relies on the geometric techniques to control the areas of the faces of the force diagram. For instance, in the *Hedracrete* project, changing the areas of the rectangular faces to zero in the force diagram releases the structure from the lateral support on the top chord and results in the top members to go into tension. Consequently, this method allows us to explore the realm of architectural structures with combined tension and compressive forces with full control over the geometry and the force equilibrium in the system.

— Masoud Akbarzadeh

2002 Serpentine Pavilion by Toyo Ito and Cecil Balmond. Image courtesy of Balmond Studio.

Breaking the Box

Connect half the side of a square to an
adjacent third—and repeat … repeat …
cut and bend, then fill in the alternate
voids—a Pavilion!

— Cecil Balmond

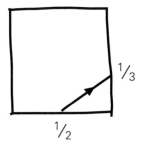

The Great Court at the British Museum. Photograph by Ed Webster.

Serendipity

The word "dumbness" is not much used in the UK, we use the word "stupidity." We assume that dumb means the same as stupid, but sugar coated, with the hard edge of the pejorative connotation removed. We also use the word dumb to mean mute, lacking the power of speech, and so we find it offensive to use it to mean stupid.

It is difficult to see how stupidity can solve the overwhelming problems the world faces from global warming to never-ending conflict and the appalling disparity between the rich and the poor, when it caused them in the first place.

Serendipity is another matter. Serendipity means making happy and unexpected discoveries by accident, such as the discovery of penicillin by Alexander Fleming or vulcanised rubber by Charles Goodyear. Fleming and Goodyear were anything but stupid and they were able to see the ramifications of what happened by chance in the petri dish or on the hot stove.

When I generated the geometry of the roof of the British Museum Great Court by Foster + Partners and Buro Happold, constructed by Waagner Biro, I was not aware that the roof members would create curves that are tangent to the pediments over the porticos. I was aware of the pediments in as much as they required a certain clearance, but that was it. It's possible that Filomena Russo who did much of the design at Foster + Partners was aware of the tangency, but I don't remember ever discussing it with Filo. I suppose that is serendipity.

— Chris Williams

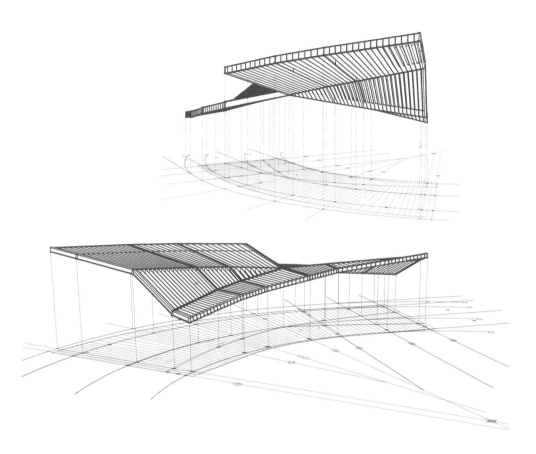

The W-house has a ruled surface roof which was built using normative construction techniques.

Challengers

When launching a creative practice, discussion quickly turned to questions of how to execute ambitious formal designs without incurring huge expenses for clients that were reticent to hire a young design firm in the first place. The dumbest, but smartest answer became the driving force for many of the early projects executed—to work within normative construction systems but strategically challenge those normative approaches where they could be tweaked to elicit formal or material effects.

The ruled surface was not a new idea but had been largely used in constructing formwork or hyperbolic shapes where every member is straight. However, we saw it as a technique that could easily be applied to normative stick construction. If one can reduce the complexity in the project to edge beams, typical stick-framing systems could be used to construct complex shapes while staying within the existing economic models of the builders. Early designs explored different ways of constructing edges from CNC-milled and laminated plywood to curved steel w-sections to simple bent dimensional lumber as top plates of support walls. There were also projects that played with challenging the normative spacing of the ruled stick members to vary the geometry and resulting architectural effects further.

The W-house was one of the most ambitious as the roof was split and shaped in response to the landscape and environmental features. Complex edge beam assemblies were fabricated in machine shops and geolocated on site. Once those elements were properly situated, the "dumbness" of the normative stick-construction system was easily integrated with the "smartness" embodied in the machine shop fabricated elements.

— Jefferson Ellinger

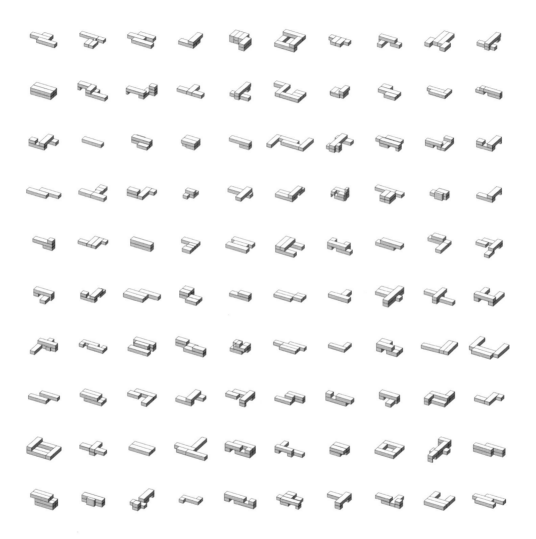

The Modern Modular Unlimited 3D Variations by Resolution: 4 Architecture.

What Is the Dumbest, but Smartest Thing You've Done?

Building Blocks

For over 100 years, architects have pursued the Holy Grail of modernism, which is to design a relatively affordable, modern domestic space that could be mass-produced.

Although the single-family home has historically been a focal point in the exploration of architectural ideas, most people do not live in a home designed by an architect. In fact, most domestic structures are conceived by developers as products, produced for profit. The efficiency of mass-production, both conceptually and physically, has in many ways contributed to the self-same tombstones representing graveyards of complacency, otherwise known as the American suburb.

Numerous academic attempts at mass-production were generally devised as products with a high level of design, but often were burdened by inventing complicated manufacturing processes. Conversely, commercial attempts were more successful in efficient and feasible manufacturing processes, but they were limited in their homes' design flexibility— seemingly strangled by the measures of production.

As an alternative to designing a product, we have been exploring a process; a method of design that worked within the limits of the industry to leverage existing modes of residential prefabrication.

The majority of residential modular manufacturers in the United States use a standard maximum width of 16 feet, based on Department of Transportation highway shipping regulations. Although module lengths vary by factory, the most common length is 60 feet, because it fills a line space in the assembly process, making it the most cost-efficient dimension. Within these parameters, we found a kindred spirit. Having completed renovations of long, linear loft spaces in New York City, thinking inside the box was a natural extension of our practice.

These modules, derived from established dimensional constraints, became the conceptual "building blocks" of a simple design strategy.

The building blocks—designed from the inside out—can be arranged in response to any specific program and site requirements. The compositions produced by this volumetric exercise are analogous to the toy blocks of a child, but the resultant limitless variations represent the potential of the system. The building blocks developed into a range of customizable typologies and evolved into the basis of our methodology of design—*The Modern Modular*.

— Joseph Tanney

25 identical wall tiles which give the illusion of variation by David Riebe of Windsor Fiberglass.

What Is the Dumbest, but Smartest Thing You've Done?

Dumb(ness) Rules

Ten years ago, I made a life decision to leave architecture. I left an academic position and for the most part my engagement with the practice of architecture. My new job was to learn how to manage and run an established composites manufacturing company. The new company is a production shop, meaning it makes the same things over and over from a limited set of molds, relying on the repetition of parts, a world where deviation and difference is most often the result of mishap and not the desired outcome. This is different than a job shop, which takes on discrete projects, generates new parts, and sees them through to completion. Everything about my architectural background suggested I should be running a job shop.

After a few years, when I became comfortable with my knowledge of the material system, and learned for the most part how to run a business for profit, it was time to address the larger challenges. How to find new opportunities for discovery within the constant repetition of our production lines. It was time to act like an architect again. After numerous failed attempts at trying to make tooling more parametric, I realized that it was beyond my ability to transform our permanent physical tools into algorithmic scripts.

What emerged was a focus on repetition as a system to operate within. This trajectory required much more discipline in the investigations. In retrospect, I think the origins of my developing line of inquiry came from a series of drawing exercises I gave my first-year design students 15 years ago. The exercises were inspired by Ken Warriner and sought to explore simple rule-based constructions that were intended to discover thresholds between fixed, stable, given; and emergent, indeterminate, transformative conditions. How could a simple set of lines or rules, be *both* knowable *and* unknowable simultaneously.

The composite tiles shown here are the results of an interest in the graphic quality of tree bark. I designed one dumb unit based upon two sets of really simple rules. This created the limits within which I was able to search for that threshold condition, *both and*. The result is a single unit that when populated visually creates a dynamic and changing field. At the time, these introductory drawing exercises seemed minor in consequence to the five-year course of study for architecture students, but these dumb little assignments now shape and define much of the expanded capacity of our shop.

— David Riebe

Prototype of a hexagonal façade panel *HexChar* formed with carbon negative material by Made of Air.

What Is the Dumbest, but Smartest Thing You've Done?

Carbon Sink Marks

The Smart Materials wave in the early 2000s London architecture scene appeared in my inbox in the form of a never-published, but well circulated 300-page PDF sent by a friend. This definition of "smart" applied to materials had me re-focusing my lens on the city, and assigning quick values to surfaces and structures that were either doing a job, or sitting around, standing by. Smart, having a near association to active, hinted at a kind of intelligence, a feedback system with the environment. As a counterpoint, "dumbness" would be nearer to inert: those walls, bricks, and roads that formed a traditional European city, solidly built for purpose, standing by for millennia.

In 2011, we presented our idea for a new composite (Made of Air) as a base material for building products. Composed of waste CO_2 from the atmosphere, the material reduces more CO_2 than is generated in its production, rendering it carbon negative. It's ability to store atmospheric carbon enables building products, and thereby cities, to act as engineered carbon sinks.

The skipping and linking of industries and processes needed to make this happen is smart, motivated in part by a hyper multidisciplinarity that grew out of my architecture training, an aversion to settling into a profession.

The material, by my early 2000s definition, is dumb.

Once it's composition into granules is complete, there is no further surface activity. As a thermoplastic, it is formable into multiple products, and, once applied to a building, inert. In fact, it's principle job is to store carbon, stoically, for millennia. Unresponsive to any further climatic activity, the material itself is a tomb that manages the end of the carbon cycle, retiring the CO_2 pumped into the atmosphere since the Industrial Revolution, to the earth, with a carbon removal certificate issued to the building owner on the way down.

— Allison Dring

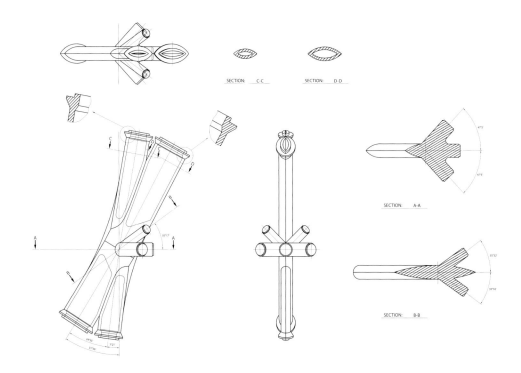

Shop drawings for the oculus intersection on the Taichung Tropical Rainforest Greenhouse.

What Is the Dumbest, but Smartest Thing You've Done?

Warped Transitions

The smartest dumb thing that I've done (and I've done many so it was hard to choose one) was while leading the design of the Taichung Tropical Rainforest Greenhouse 25 years ago I asked the steel fabricators to develop simple "railroad board" physical models of the joint castings to add modeling clay for smoothing out the transitions between the different forms. The addition of these warped surfaces was not required for the structural performance because the engineering performance and metallurgical casting constraints could be resolved without them, but I dumbly wanted these "ornamental" warped transitions to harmonize with the spirit of the exposed structure architecture. Even with the language barrier (maybe this is a case of it helping), we effectively communicated my desire to have warped surface transitions between the ocular column sections and thick plate forms.

Back then, we were stuck trying to figure out how to add this to the fabrication shop drawings. The fabricator in Kaohsiung mailed photographs of the models (white railroad board with green modeling clay for the warped transitions) to my office in NYC and I faxed back my approval with some requests for slight adjustments. I was delighted with the process and the results. Fast forward to today and there are now many readily available software tools to document these warped transitions, but I suspect that the software or scripting of mathematics based forms would control the surface definition based upon the code and the user's expertise. Our approach for the Taichung castings is sculptural rather than mathematically based and produces a much more natural essence that, in my dumb opinion, is infinitely more beautiful.

— Bruce Danziger

Kanno Museum by Atelier Hitoshi Abe. Photograph by Daici Ano.

Cardboard

Kanno Museum is a private art gallery, located on a hilly site of a small town, with a view on the Pacific Ocean. Within 10mx12mx10m volume, we have decided to give architecture a form by creating eight spaces to hold eight sculptures. The cells that constitute each of these rooms are made of steel plates 3.2mm thick, with about 25 embossed protuberances per square meter.

As with every other project, we have approached the design through the most conventional tool for study and representation of ideas—we made a cardboard model. This time, however, we have decided to allow the representation to determine the approach, which, at first seemed like a naïve idea. The model was defined by balancing the conditions of cardboard surfaces of each cell, which were formed by the internal pressure of the small spaces within the large space of the entire building. Properties of the material and the structural representation shown by the model drove us to the realization that we could literally translate the object of representation into the building design. Enthusiastically, we dove into the experiment of leaping over the conventional sequence in the design approach taking a direct jump from the model to the building. The cardboard model allowed for the language through which techniques came to be articulated. Cardboard walls of the model became the honeycomb panels in the building, formed by welding the embossed protuberances of the two steel panels, resulting in this unusual "steel cardboard" structure that was only possible to be unfolded by this bold leap in the design process.

— Hitoshi Abe

St. Nicholas Antiochian Orthodox Christian Church by Marlon Blackwell Architects. Photograph by Timothy Hursley.

The Smartest Dumb Thing

Our design for the 2009 St. Nicholas Antiochian Orthodox Christian Church along the interstate highway in Springdale Arkansas—an adaptive reuse and addition to an existing welding shed was about to begin construction. It is a simple white metal-clad box with profile at the front façade facing west toward the highway. The color white represented the sacredness of the church seen from all directions, but for me it seemed too much of its place even confused with the detritus of nearby metal buildings in this ruburban context. What else could I do? Our very modest budget of $100 per square foot was already maxed out. Making a quick outline perspective sketch on white copy paper I colored in the other building façades except for the front façade and then outlined the perimeter of the new two-dimensional face with a heavier line, finally drawing a dark colored band around the base of the building. Pow! A banal box is transformed. The color of the front façade metal cladding remains white but all other façades are changed to dark bronze and the same color trim is used to outline the perimeter of the front façade, together with a 4'-wide band of blackened wood chips around the building base, the church separates from the prosaic world around it. A sacred visage for the church emerges as both façade and billboard providing an iconic abstract figure in a landscape of unholy unions.

No costs. No delays. And to date one of our most internationally recognized projects.

— Marlon Blackwell

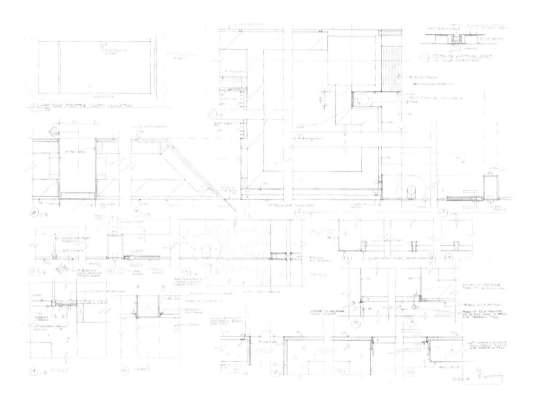

Miscellaneous details—RMIT Design Hub by Sean Godsell Architects.

The Dumbest Mistake

In this digital age architects are tricked into believing that their computer-generated drawings, accurate to the millimeter, can also be built to the same degree of precision. CAD drawing programs remove the implied construction tolerances that existed in the era of hand drawn details. When I detail (still by hand, although my office uses the computer) I draw as if I'm building and with the knowledge that construction, unlike CAD documentation, is by definition imprecise because it requires "error" (in the form of tolerances) as part of its lexicon. In Australia we dimension in millimeters— for example "300" equals 0.3 meters. A foot is 304.8mm. Try building to a fraction of a millimeter—it's not possible. Contractors are left with the responsibility of translating the architect's drawing into something practical. We are light years removed from the architect as artisan.

Any architect who still details and has their detail built knows that errors occur on site regularly. It simply goes with the territory. Construction programs, cost, and other mitigating factors deny the architect the right to demand that things be built "to the millimeter," and the real art of architecture exists in the architect's ability to embrace errors; to "adapt and overcome" to quote the US marines and to still control built outcomes so that only those intimately involved in the delivery of the building know where a detail deviates from the original documentation. My best details are those drawn with a carpenter's pencil on drywall in discussion with those workers directly involved in the resolution and delivery of the particular detail in question. This is the artifice of architecture. The dumbest mistake that one can make is to not understand that this is an essential part of what we do.

— Sean Godsell

Point House by MacKay-Lyons Sweetapple Architects.
Photograph by Matthew MacKay-Lyons.

Zero Detailing

In a PBS special on our work (Design E2, The Village Architect), Kenneth Frampton describes our architecture as "banal." He goes on to say that when you achieve the banal, the building looks like it was always there.

Cultures are smart—individuals, not so much. I'm infatuated with the vernacular, or *Architecture Without Architects* (following Bernard Rudofsky). All models of sustainable architecture are found in vernacular building traditions. The vernacular is what you do when you can't afford to get it wrong.

Many sustainable building design practices grow out of a deep understanding of the specifics of climate and material culture, often producing counter-intuitive solutions. For example, the Point House employs zero eaves, or no roof overhang. On the South Shore of Nova Scotia, with 260 freeze-thaw cycles a year, overhangs create ice dams and leaky buildings.

So, one person's banal is another's minimalism.

— Brian MacKay-Lyons

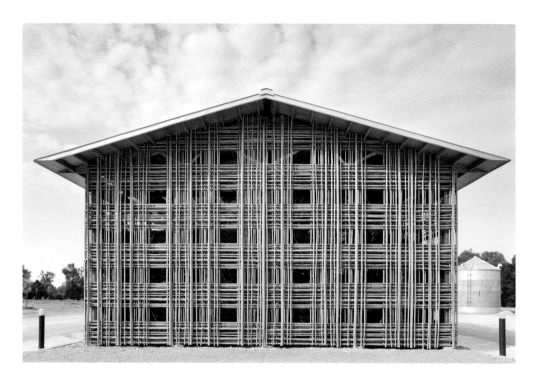

Barn B at Mason Lane Farm by de Leon & Primmer Architecture Workshop. Photograph by Roberto de Leon.

Accidental Tradition

The bamboo lattice façade of Barn B at Mason Lane Farm has a deceptively simple installation technique developed through a full-scale mockup. Originally detailed to have the stalks be individually attached with metal screws, it quickly became apparent that this method would be too challenging since bamboo has a particularly hard surface that is prone to cracking and shrinking as it dries. This necessitated that all the screws would have had to be carefully pre-drilled, a time-consuming and tedious process. We realized that we could not think about bamboo in the same way as ordinary wood-barn siding.

We ultimately stumbled upon a low-tech and efficient lashing technique. Using common galvanized wire ties—the same type that you would use to install rebar—multiple stalks of bamboo were bundled together and attached to the primary barn frame. The wire ties were then hand twisted with an awl to tighten these bundles, a feature which allowed for periodic re-tightening over time as the stalks dried. This lashing technique produced an interesting micro-detail in the façade that is only visible at close range—a series of extended wire loops.

In hindsight, we realized that we had unintentionally and serendipitously reinterpreted a traditional cord lashing technique often applied to bamboo!

— Roberto de Leon
— Ross Primmer

Photograph by Paul Yaggie.

What Is the Dumbest, but Smartest Thing You've Done?

Dumbing Up

It would be difficult to account for all the dumb things that I've done, but easy to list the few that I've "accomplished." In our landscape architecture studio, we use the term dumb rather often—always in an aspirational way. Seeking dumbness is a tribute to farmers and others who, by necessity, shaped places in practical and economical ways. Achieving a dumb landscape design results from either letting the obvious happen, or through the rigor of drubbing the design out of something—to discover its essence. To us, there is no dumbing down: "dumb" leads to simple, functional, economical, and lasting landscapes.

— Michael Boucher

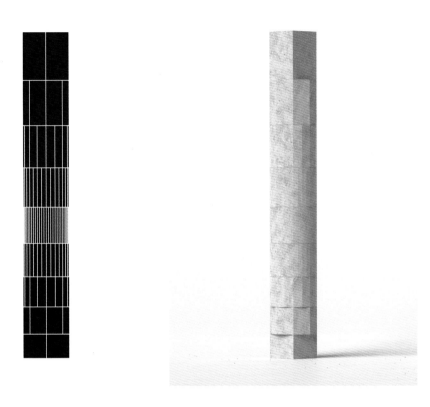

Column with entasis.

What Is the Dumbest, but Smartest Thing You've Done?

Silent Form

We design things that
are inert and silent.

Things offering a blank
expression, a static gaze.

Things deliberate in their
slow reveal of influence
and reason.

— William O'Brien Jr.

A, B 1:2 at Rice University School of Architecture. Photograph by Nash Baker.

What Is the Dumbest, but Smartest Thing You've Done?

Soft Focus

The photograph's ability to remove a viewer from the interferences of moving light allows it to rely on other means to convey depth. The shifting scales of perspective, the blurring of distant objects, and contrasts in light and shade can create the perception of deep space. *A, B 1:2* explores some of these devices through the installation of a building inside another building.

Traditional domestic spaces rely on material difference to define boundaries whereas *A, B 1:2* is uniformly colored to probe what space-making potentials lie in changing levels of detail. The faces of the house's all-gray interior are creased and pleated like a spool of cloth. Shadows cast by folded surfaces render the interior in varying degrees of exactness, creating multiple areas of focus, or depths of field. Boundaries between levels of detail are designed with an image-construction technique that mines a photograph for changes in color, brightness, and clarity. In its translation across scales and from two to three dimensions, the project finds ways to render familiar objects (window dressings, furniture, finishes, etc.) as both articulate and dumb.

— Michelle Chang

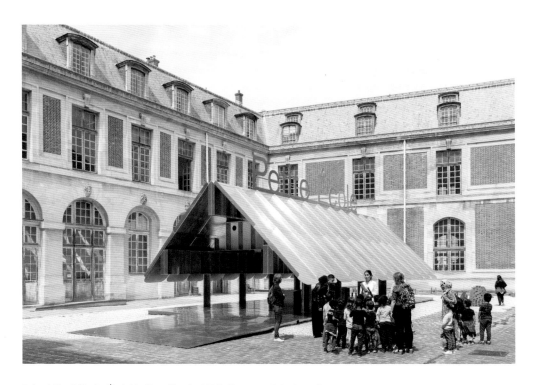

School No. 3 (Petite École) in Versailles by MOS. Photograph by Iwan Baan.

Dumb Architecture

We like dumb architecture. We dislike clever architecture. Dumb architecture is about buildings. Dumb architecture is not about ideas. It likes things. It makes drawings and models. It stares at you blankly in photos. It's not about the cutting edge or the next big gizmo. And it's obviously not about smartness, or whatever. It's dumb, not stupid. It's crude, not elegant. It's beautiful. It finds beauty everywhere. With dumb architecture, what you see is what you get. It makes due with what's around it. It's not critical, or discriminating, or sophisticated, or articulate. Dumb architecture isn't very interested in expressing itself. It prefers to not say too much. When you ask it a question it speaks matter-of-factly. It's direct. It's not self-conscious. But it's not too confident. At home it sits in its pajamas watching strange how-to tutorials, again, instead of the latest breaking news. It prefers slapstick humor to monologues. It prefers simple shapes and whole numbers. It's not quote-unquote designed. It's not original, or unfamiliar, or shockingly new. It doesn't care if it makes sense. And it doesn't mind being wrong. It marches to the beat of its own drum. It won't get upset at misreadings. It doesn't hold a grudge. It repeats itself on occasion, a lot. It says the same thing twice or more. Dumb architecture is generous. It's endearing. It's not tragic. It's not heavy. It's happy. It's playful. It's childish. It's

— Hilary Sample
— Michael Meredith

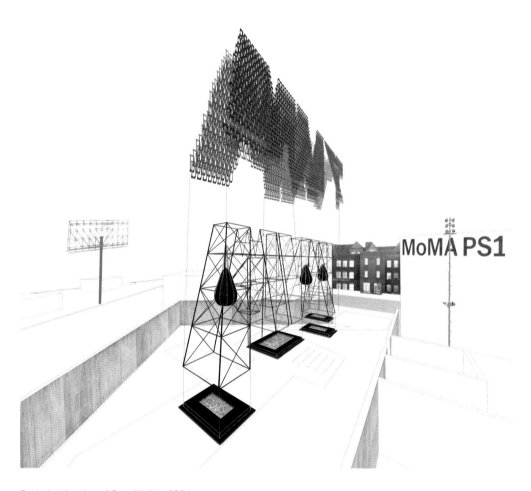

Exploded drawing of *Party Wall* by CODA.

What Is the Dumbest, but Smartest Thing You've Done?

"Yes, I Will, Yes"

Peter Eisenman once quipped that architecture should be more like the work of James Joyce than Britney Spears. By this, of course, he meant that architecture should be aimed at an elite, architecturally literate audience, and require close reading in order to decipher its meaning, rather than simply communicating a simplistic one-liner to a mass populous. My inside knowledge of certain Irish dialects gave me a particular vantage point on this statement. In fact, I do not believe that Joyce's prose necessitates close reading. In fact, what is difficult about it is that it is, at times, the spoken (or even thought) word in a written form. Molly Bloom's "Yes I said yes I will Yes" may, to some readers, appear poetic, and to others, simply a Dublin way to say "Hell, Yes!" In other words, James Joyce is also Britney Spears. Or, dumb and smart. I wondered if architecture too could communicate several layers of ideas to various audiences.

Party Wall, the MoMA PS1 pavilion in 2013 cuts a linear line that both divides and unites the former school's series of courtyards. From a certain distance, it is clear that the form of the 120'-long and 40'-tall installation has a word-like form, but in looking at the object, it is not clear what that word might be. The pavilion, as both an architectural and literal sign does not communicate by itself but relies directly on its context to produce a hint of its true meaning: under certain lighting conditions, at certain times of day, at certain times of year, the clue to understanding the concept appears as a shadow in text on the ground. Read: WALL.

A continuous linear element, *Party Wall* is all-wall at the top, but at the bottom it stands on four splayed feet. When coupled with the slightly larger context of billboards and signs that proliferate like grazing beasts around the site, the object becomes more sign than wall; a sign that, by its own definition, points to something other than itself. The play between thing itself, sign and signified, is tossed back and forth. It represents a progression that extends beyond both semantic duck and syntactic domino.

At the finer scale, the weaving together of longboard off-cuts into a pattern sets up a similar tension at the level of the façade. Mounted on base of the façade, the solid boards afford enclosure and architectural pediment. When removed, they afford sitting (with legs, we call them benches) or play (with "soft-trucks" they revert to a strange kind of skateboard).

This work is the first in a line of dumb-smart works that aim at a popular and elite audience simultaneously.

— Caroline O'Donnell

The Hulse Pavilion by Anthony Ames Architect. Photograph by Chuck Pittman.

My Favorite Mistake

The important thing is to have an idea. There are no dumb ideas—only dumb architects. It is highly preferable to have a dumb idea and a smart architect than the other way around. Three of the most significant buildings of the twentieth century began as dumb ideas—Corb's Villa Savoye—a house raised on columns, the Leicester University Engineering Building by James Stirling—a tiny high rise with a water tank on top—and the Farnsworth House by Mies—a house with perimeter glass walls. However, because these buildings had smart architects they all became architectural icons and good ideas. I had a dumb idea once—back in the '70s. My first commission was for a small guest house / pool house—the Hulse Pavilion. I had recently acquired a publication—*Five Architects*—which introduced me to the work of a group of five architects practicing in New York City (Peter Eisenman, Michael Graves, Charles Gwathmey, John Hejduk, and Richard Meier—see Google) who believed in and promoted an architecture based loosely on the second coming of the modern movement but more specifically on Le Corbusier's white villas of the 1920s. My idea was to appropriate their aesthetic in my first commission—not in homage, which might have been a good idea, but through mimicry—which was a dumb idea. In retrospect I used *Five Architects* as an architectural treatise—sort of like

Serlio and Palladio—but again, through simulation rather than through applied theory. The Hulse Pavilion imitated Richard Meier's Smith House—closed entry façade, open and glazed rear elevation. The entry was through a dense poche into a double-height living space overlooking a body of water—in the Smith House the body of water is the Long Island Sound in the Hulse Pavilion it was a swimming pool. The house incorporated the smooth, curvilinear planes and volumes of Gwathmey's suave and eloquent Hampton's houses. I was influenced by Peter Eisenman's geometric compositions generated by analysis (not psychoanalysis) and an obsession with Terragni. The plan and the rear elevation at Hulse are the same—a rectangle generated by the drop-down diagonal of the square. This glazed white box was attached to an expressive white wall inspired by the architecture of John Hejduk in his wall houses. All of this was achieved with cognizance of the Hanselmann House by Michael Graves—possibly the finest example of a dumb / smart idea in the history of 20th-century architecture. The Hulse Pavilion ended up receiving its share of acclaim and was widely published. This led to several commissions—even though it was a dumb idea.

— Anthony Ames

Sectional model, House on a Slope. Photography by KARAMUK KUO.

Dumb Rules!

Very often we find ourselves fighting the shackles of codes and regulations, twisting like contortionists in the effort to avoid being mundane and perfunctory. But sometimes, the most unexpected, the most radical, is also the dumbest thing to do.

In many Swiss cantons, the maximum height of the allowable building envelope is defined by a parallel offset of the existing terrain. Not so surprising on a flat site but can be bizarre on a sloped site. Of course, nobody ever takes this literally since, as architects, we often want to feel in control of the form. And so, we often forego the maximum in search of a happy compromise. For example, in the case of housing when building on a slope, the dominant typology is a terraced parti with apartments arranged on single floors. The stepping of the floors approximates the slope of the hypothetical envelope. Everyone gets a view, nobody questions anything.

But the terraced housing is also a one liner. It sacrifices many other qualities for the all-important view. Typological variety, multiple exposures, spatial and formal expressions all become suppressed in favor of *the view*. It's all about the same-same.

With the House on a Slope, we did the dumbest thing possible. We simply followed the code (yes, literally!)—taking the slope to define the ridge line of the gable roof. And then we even extended it further, cantilevering the roof to claim some outdoor space under the shade—an attenuated threshold. The envelope was maximized even further through this borrowed space.

The gable roof sneaks a five-unit apartment building into a single-family villa neighborhood while its slope and its giant overhang gives it a distinguished character, subverting the norm. Nestled inside this form are five radically different apartments, each having a view, each having an outdoor space. And each having a unique spatial characteristic celebrating the diversity of lifestyles possible.

Sometimes following the rules is the most rebellious thing to do.

— Jeannette Kuo

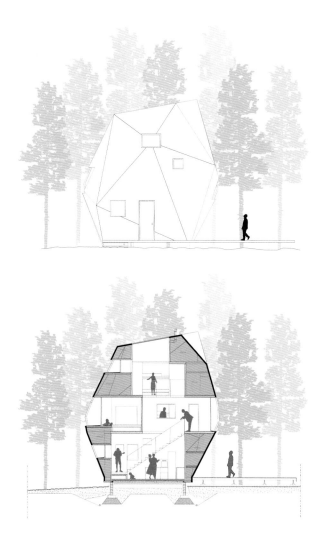

Meteorite elevation and section by Ateljé Sotamaa.

The Misfit

I believe organizational strategies for buildings should work like "dumb" recipes. The Misfit is my favorite example of such a recipe. It goes like this: Combine two forms, which don't fit together and voilá, a third, interstitial form emerges filled with unexpected, exciting possibilities for architecture.

One of the two forms could be a constellation of interior spaces. It can address the more intricate programmatic requirements and human scale. The other form could be the exterior. It can address, for example, the city, the landscape, and the crowd. The two combined will always generate an interstitial space, usually with refreshingly unexpected possibilities for use.

The scale of the building will determine the range of possibilities for the interstitial space, also referred to as poché in architectural discourse. It could be occupied by public space like the Jean Nouvel and Philippe Starck unrealized Tokyo Opera House, or filled with artwork like the John Soane's House in London.

The Misfit strategy is dumb in terms of its straightforward approach to program and brilliant in terms the efficiency with which it generates collateral architectural opportunities.

One of my favorite qualities of the Misfit recipe is that it creates a dramaturgical sequence of experiences rather than being phenomenologically transparent. In other words, the view of the exterior does not reveal the logic of the interior but instead creates an experience in dramaturgical contrast to the interior.

The Meteorite is a three-story residential wood building we designed with the Misfit recipe: The first form is a folded monolithic shape on the outside, which addresses the scale of the forest. The second form is an intricate arrangement of rooms and voids on the interior. The two combined generate a poché. The air in the poché acts as insulation for the mass timber building and contains occupiable nooks and crannies, inbuilt art displays, storage, and technical systems, all which can be easily accessed and maintained.

What is wonderful about a dumb recipe in organizing a project like the Meteorite is that I can focus my energy on tweaking what it generates to perfection. I can explore the nuances of form, intricacies of structure, sensibilities of materiality, and issues of representation, atmosphere, and aesthetics. A simple recipe, or algorithm to use another term, effortlessly organizes a building and creates a solid point of departure for designing terrific architecture.

— Kivi Sotamaa

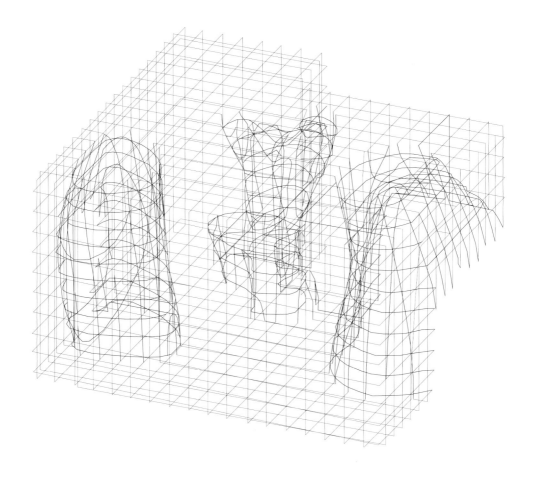

Process drawing of Loewy books by artists bookshop by Jakob + MacFarlane.

How Dumb Became Smart

In an early work of our studio in 2000 for a bookshop in Paris we were agonizing over how to find an idea for a very small project that could be a system and a set of independent parts.

We needed to create a space to show, store, and for the sale of books in the same tiny space—many things that were somehow unrelated. At a critical moment it seemed impossible to move forward. We had the parts but no overall meaning. Out of frustration we kind of abandoned the seriousness of the problem and imagined a dumb idea—a bookshop made of books.

We enthusiastically went into creating the whole volume of our given space and completely filling it with books—creating an impossible situation—and from this we imagined and cut into this volume to create new wild pathways, boring into this solid of books. When we had finished, we had something but not a bookshop. We then went back to getting rid of the books making shelves in their place. A dumb idea had just led us to a very smart one. From this dumb response to this problem we went on to create an important part of our work.

— Dominique Jakob
— Brendan MacFarlane

The Ex of In house was built with local materials in 11 months by five craftsmen led by Javier Gomez. The house is heated and cooled via geothermal well. Photograph by Paul Warchol.

**Seven Point Manifesto
for Explorations of In**

The seven point manifesto
underlies a 913-square-foot house:

1. To study architecture freed
   from the purely objective.

2. From origins of architecture
   we explore In.

3. In: All space is sacred space.

4. The architecture of In
   dominates space via space.

5. Intrinsic In is an elemental
   force of sensual beauty.

6. In is useless, but in the future
   will be used. Purpose finds In.

7. The thing containing is
   not the thing contained.

— Steven Holl
— Dimitra Tsachrelia

Pole Dance by SO – IL.

The Scramble Manifesto

We like the idea but have just gone over
our calendar—and literally the only day
we have available till mid-January is
Christmas Eve. So possibly the dumbest
but smartest thing we have done is
becoming architects in the first place.
Dumbest because it requires so much
time, smartest because it offers so
much joy.

— Florian Idenburg
— Jing Liu

"But in fact it was always unfinished — it could always change: adding other structures and reducing some, throughout its life."

— Cedric Price, 2000

It Is What It Is

Although the title of this manifesto sounds like it is against intelligence, that is quite the contrary. If anything, it was intended to question: What truly is intelligence? Often times, artificial intelligence is thought of as being smart but rarely is the word "intelligence" precisely defined. I've heard the broken record about computers calculating beyond human comprehension. Then someone predictably argues that humans are more creative than machines. Another may respond with: What really is creativity? Asking questions is an inherent trait of being human. We like asking questions and we usually like (even better) to find an answer. However, many times there is more than one answer.

This manifesto started with a question, which led to another question, which concluded with over 50 unique responses. It's been an evocative intellectual journey, where in many ways the manifesto is like the Sol LeWitt drawing. Each person traces a line with their hand ... leading to something other than where it started ... but resulting in something with a rhythmic uniformity. It's really just a story about how a simple "dumb" question provided a lens to understand the culture of contemporary architecture. It is clear, there are many possible futures. In many ways, this manifesto scratches at the essence of design and architecture. Fundamentally, acting "smartly dumb" is just another way of saying "rigorous."

Karatsu Style (Rice Bale Shape) Flower Vase by Takashi Nakazato. Stoneware, Wood Fired. Made in Japan.
Kintsugi Restoration by Gen Saratani and his assistants. Urushi Lacquer, Gold Powder. Restoration in New York.
Photograph by Naoki Uemura / Sara Japanese Pottery.

Acknowledgments

To the contributors. This book would not have been possible without your thoughtful responses. Like a flower vase that has been broken and put back together precisely, this book is both a manifesto and anti-manifesto simultaneously.

To Gordon Goff, Publisher at ORO Editions, who instantly supported this book project without hesitation.

To M. Wesam Al Asali, for encouraging me to start this project.

To my wife and partner in life, Ting-Ting, who always puts up with my "dumb" stuff.

To my daughters, Amelia and Sophie. Providing endless healthy distractions while teaching me to see the world (yet again) through the lens of play, joy, and novelty.

To Dad, for teaching me the rigor behind "the game of the least mistakes."

To Mom, for teaching me to appreciate so much that is normally taken for granted.

To any student who doesn't know where to start. You don't need a genius idea to begin, you just need to do something.

Publishers of Architecture, Art, and Design
Gordon Goff: Publisher

www.oroeditions.com
info@oroeditions.com

Published by ORO Editions

Graphic Design: Joseph Choma
Text: Joseph Choma
ORO Project Coordinator: Jake Anderson

10 9 8 7 6 5 4 3 2 1 First Edition

Library of Congress data available upon request. World Rights: Available

ISBN: 978-1-951541-37-8

Color Separations and Printing: ORO Group Ltd.
Printed in China.

International Distribution: www.oroeditions.com/distribution

ORO Editions makes a continuous effort to minimize the overall carbon footprint of its publications. As
part of this goal, ORO Editions, in association with Global ReLeaf, arranges to plant trees to replace those
used in the manufacturing of the paper produced for its books. Global ReLeaf is an international campaign
run by American Forests, one of the world's oldest nonprofit conservation organizations. Global ReLeaf
is American Forests' education and action program that helps individuals, organizations, agencies, and
corporations improve the local and global environment by planting and caring for trees.